THE FAITH TO DOUBT

ALSO BY STEPHEN BATCHELOR

Alone With Others:
An Existential Approach to Buddhism

The Tibet Guide

TRANSLATOR

A Guide to the Bodhisattva's Way of Life
(Bodhicaryavatara)

Echoes of Voidness

Song of the Profound View

EDITOR

The Way of Korean Zen

The Jewel in the Lotus: A Guide to the
Buddhist Traditions of Tibet

THE
FAITH
TO
DOUBT

GLIMPSES OF
BUDDHIST
UNCERTAINTY

Stephen Batchelor

COUNTERPOINT · BERKELEY

Calligraphy on page 18 by Ven. Kusan Sunim
Designed and typeset by Gopa & Ted2, Inc.

Library of Congress Cataloging-in-Publication
Data is available

ISBN 978-1-61902-535-6

COUNTERPOINT
2560 Ninth Street, Suite 318
Berkeley, CA 94710
www.counterpointpress.com

Printed in the United States of America
Distributed by Publishers Group West

10 9 8 7 6 5 4 3 2 1

Contents

Preface to the New Edition

This twenty-fifth anniversary edition of *The Faith to Doubt* is a re-issue of the original 1990 Parallax Press text, which has been out of print for some years. Since Korean Buddhism is better known today than it was when the book first appeared, I have decided to change the Japanese term "Zen" for its Korean equivalent "Sŏn." I have also added an Afterword. Otherwise, the text is identical. I am most grateful to Jack Shoemaker and the staff at Counterpoint Press for making this book available to a new generation of readers.

Stephen Batchelor
Aquitaine, 2014

Preface

This short book was started during my stay in Songgwang Sa Monastery, Korea, from 1981 through 1984. It is a collection of essays, quotations, journal entries and stories strung together in an attempt to create a picture of one person's encounter with Zen Buddhism. Although chapters 3 through 7 were first drafted in Korea, chapters 1 and 2 were only written up on my return to England. Thus a varied texture of thoughts and feelings, joys and sorrows, hopes and doubts, introspective reflections and observations of the world, occasional insights and bounteous confusions are spread across these pages.

The Faith to Doubt continues an inquiry that began with my previous book *Alone With Others* (1983), which arose out of an eight-year training in the Gelugpa school of Tibetan Buddhism. I must emphasize that any reservations I may express in this work about Tibetan Buddhism are conclusions reached in the course of my own particular training and are not intended as a criticism of the Tibetan traditions as a whole, about which I have limited knowledge. There are indeed meditative systems (such as *mahamudra* and *dzog-chen*) in Tibetan Buddhism which in many respects resemble Zen. The main reason for my not having pursued those forms of meditation is given in chapter 2.

Likewise, this book is not intended to be a conclusive or a comprehensive account of Zen Buddhism. It too is a personal interpretation, largely informed by the Korean Zen tradition, in particular the branch of that tradition based on the teachings of Chinul. Above all, what I have written here is merely an account of a stage on a longer journey.

I am most grateful to the monks of Songgwang Sa Monastery for putting up with me for nearly four years and providing the peace and quiet needed to meditate, think and write. Since my return to England I have received many helpful criticisms from friends who have read various drafts. In particular I would like to thank Hans Ludin, the late Michael Campbell, Therese Fitzgerald, and Arnie Kotler for their comments. Above all I am indebted to my teacher the late Ven. Kusan Sunim, a true man of Zen. For an authoritative account of Korean Zen Buddhism, the reader is encouraged to read his book *The Way of Korean Zen* (Weatherhill, 1985).

—Stephen Batchelor Vesak, 2532 (1989)
Sharpham, Devon, England

"Ah!"

—*The Perfection of Wisdom Discourse in One Letter*

For Songil

Question and Response

The way of the Buddha is a living response to a living question. Yet whenever it has become institutionalized its vital response has become a well-formulated answer. The seemingly important task of preserving a particular set of answers often causes the very questions which gave rise to those answers to be forgotten. Then the lucid answers Buddhism provides are cut off from the stammering voice that asks the questions.

The question we ask can only be clumsily phrased in words, for our very existence declares itself to us as a question. Birth, sickness, aging, and death are the mute, imperative voices of this question that beckon us along a path. To be vital, this path can never stray from the ground of its question, it can never rest content with any answer. The path leads not to a coherent answer but to a series of responses as inarticulate as the question.

Once we find something to believe in, it is easy to forget the original question. But instead of acquiescing in the security of belief, we can intensify the sense of doubt. Belief, whether in a teacher, a doctrine, or even one's own experience, retreats from the questions behind a shield of protective views and concepts. But the person who questions lies open and exposed, prepared for the unpredictability of the moment.

Such questioning is not restricted to intellectual inquiry but engages the whole of our body and mind. "You must concentrate day and night," urges the *Gateless Gate,* "questioning yourself through every one of your 360 bones and 84,000 pores."[1]

That we are here at all is utterly uncanny yet remarkably ordinary. Our response to this paradox is the doubt that probes the mystery of which our minds are the insignificant center. Such doubt is a response that leads not to further knowledge about any particular thing but to wisdom of the whole.

How easy it is to lose ourselves in fascination with the uncanny and forget the ordinariness of it all! The daily life that goes on around us is calling for a response. The shining, inscrutable look in another's eyes beckons us along a path. Animals, birds, trees, grasses, rivers, and stones each call to us in their own mute voices. "Good snowflakes—they don't fall in any other place!" said Layman Pang.[2] Each moment a fresh and manifold situation is given to us but how often do we retreat from it? How clearly do we listen to and heed its call?

Chandrakirti describes how the joy the bodhisattva experiences upon responding to a call for help is not found even by the sage absorbed in the peace of nirvana.[3] Such a response is rooted in the heightened sense of interconnectedness with all that lives. It springs from the awareness that we are not alone, reflecting the inescapable responsibility each part of life bears towards the whole.

Compassion is the natural response to this call; for compassion lies at the heart of responsibility. We are responsible not merely for ourselves but for all that lives, for everything that is capable of calling out to us. The path of compassion means to silence the roar of our own internal chatter so as to be attentive to the gestures, hints, declarations, and appeals of others. The response that comes from such attentiveness does not proceed from a sense of what "should" or "ought" to be done, nor does it act with any thought of reward. "Although you act in this way for others," remarks Shantideva, "there is no sense of conceit or amazement. It is just like feeding yourself; you hope for nothing in return."[4] The way of the Buddha teaches the union of wisdom and compassion (corresponding to the paradoxical unity of mysterious emptiness and vivid appearances) as the most appropriate response to life. But this response is not apart from life. It has its roots in the very questions that existence poses, just as the lotus that emerges unstained by the mud out of which it grows.

The form Buddhism assumes is likewise a response to the situation in which it finds itself. No one can dictate or predict such a form; for it comes into being independent of any individual's design. Each cultural and historical occasion is a unique question that provokes a unique response. All we can do is to keep to the path that beckons. "For us, there is only the trying, the rest is not our business."[5]

2

The Faith to Doubt

Shortly after I was ordained as a Tibetan Buddhist monk, my faith in the Tibetan Buddhist tradition was put into doubt. At the time I was living in Dharamsala, North India, the home-in-exile of the Dalai Lama, where I was studying the doctrines of Indian Mahayana Buddhism under the guidance of Tibetan lamas of the Gelugpa order. This doctrinal study was neither dry nor academic—it was combined with daily meditative reflection on the themes taught, and enhanced by prayer and the recitation of tantric sadhanas involving visualization and mantras.

That summer, the institute in which I was studying hosted an insight meditation *(vipassana)* retreat led by U Goenka, the well-known Indian teacher from the Burmese tradition of U Ba Khin. The method of meditation taught by Goenka is a highly effective technique of developing concentrated mindfulness of body-sensations and feelings, viewed in their aspects of being impermanent, unsatisfactory, and selfless. This retreat had an overwhelming impact on me. Within the short period of ten days my consciousness was unquestionably altered, and I gained direct experiential insights into the meaning of the Buddhist teachings unlike anything I had ever realized through the methods taught by my Tibetan teachers.

This experience made me question some of the basic claims of the Tibetan lamas. The Tibetans maintain that their tradition alone preserves all the teachings of Buddhism: Hinayana, Mahayana, and Vajrayana. Goenka referred to the Buddha's *Discourse on the Foundations of Mindfulness (Satipatthana Sutta)* as the basis for much of what he taught, in particular the famous line: "This is the only way, Bhik-khus, for the purification of beings, for the overcoming of sorrow and lamentation, for the destruction of suffering and grief, for reaching the right path, for the attainment of Nibbana, namely the four foundations of mindfulness."[1] If the Tibetan claim were correct, then this statement should be able to be corroborated by the Tibetan translation of the discourse. But this basic text, which exists in Pali and in a Chinese translation from a lost Sanskrit version, was never translated into Tibetan.

Moreover, such systematic practice of mindfulness was not preserved in the Tibetan traditions. The Gelugpa lamas know about such methods and can point to long descriptions of mindfulness in their *Abhidharma* works, but the living application of the practice has largely been lost. (Only in *dzog-chen,* with the idea of "awareness" (*rig.pa.*) do we find something similar.) For many Tibetans the very term "mindfulness" *(sati* in Pali), rendered in Tibetan by *dran.pa.,* has come to be understood almost exclusively as "memory" or "recollection."

Around this time I also came across the Buddha's exhortations in the *Discourse to the Kalamas (Kalama Sutta),* which was likewise not translated into Tibetan. "Yes, Kalamas," declared the Buddha, "it is proper that you have doubt, that you have perplexity, for a doubt has arisen in a matter which is doubtful. Now, look you Kalamas, do not be led by reports, or tradition, or hearsay. Be not led by the authority of religious texts, nor by mere logic or inference, nor by considering appearances, nor by the delight in speculative opinions, nor by seeming possibilities, nor by the idea: 'this is our teacher.' But, O Kalamas, when you know for yourselves that certain things are unwholesome and wrong, and bad, then give them up . . . And when you know for yourselves that certain things are wholesome and good, then accept them and follow them."[2]

Just as Tibet was a country sealed off both by its geography and its political intentions, so is Tibetan Buddhism a sealed, hermetic system of thought and practice that makes excellent sense if studied in its own terms but gets problematic if looked at from outside its own parameters. One of the main aims of the lamas is to convince the student to take the leap of faith from the outside into the interior. Once inside the system, there is no room for doubt. The teacher is enlightened, the path complete and perfect. Everything you need to know has been accounted for; it is just a matter of putting the teachings into practice. My newly found commitment to the practice of mindfulness put at least one of my feet on the outside again, and consequently I gained the security to entertain doubts. Although my Tibetan preceptors did not encourage this interest, they did tolerate it; after all, it was another form of Buddhism. For myself, I felt stronger in my Buddhist faith, but this very strength started to undermine my need to feel devoted to any one of its many traditions.

Shortly before I left Dharamsala I had an experience that I would hesitate to call mystical, but for which I can find no better term. This is how I wrote it down: I was walking through a pine forest, returning to my hut along a narrow path trodden into the steep slope of the hillside. I struggled forward carrying a blue plastic bucket filled with fresh water that I had just collected from a source at the upper end of the valley. I was then suddenly brought to a halt by the up-surge of an overwhelming sense of the sheer mystery of everything. It was as though I were lifted up onto the crest of a shivering wave which abruptly swelled from the ocean that was life itself. How is it that people can be unaware of this most obvious question? I asked myself. How can any-one pass their life without responding to it? This experience lasted in its full intensity for only a few minutes. It was not an illumination in which some final, mystical truth became momentarily very clear. For it gave me no answers. It only revealed the massiveness of the question.

From that time on my practice of Buddhism has been one of unravelling the perception of life and the world revealed in those moments. One thing that became abundantly clear to me then was that the Buddhist path was only a means to an end. As in the beautiful parable of the raft, the Dharma is merely a temporary device to get you from one side of a river to another. Its meaning is completely distorted if it is raised to the status of an end in itself. For myself, the end for which the Buddhist path is a means can only be the penetration of this mystery of being thrown into birth only to be ejected again at death.

As hard as I tried, I could not find any teachings in Tibetan Buddhism that acknowledged or spoke of this kind of experience. The first thing I realized was that the Tibetan language did not have the capacity to express such ideas. I could find no way in Tibetan to express: "I experienced all things to be essentially mysterious" or "life is a question demanding a response." Above all I could find no way to talk of doubt as the radical basis of spiritual life. Initially, I presumed that my knowledge of the Tibetan language was insufficient. So I continued studying it in the hope of gaining the proficiency needed to express these questions.

I had consciously started my studies of classical and colloquial Tibetan with the aim of being able to ask the lamas whatever questions I wanted. What I discovered was that this was an unrealizable goal. There are some things that simply cannot be expressed in Tibetan. "Alienation," for example, makes perfect sense for a Westerner, but try and get the idea across to a Tibetan lama. Yet what I discovered from learning a language as distant from my own as Tibetan was perhaps more important. I discovered the limits of a language, the limits of a way of thinking; I discovered *what questions could and what questions could not be asked.*

In spite of these growing doubts, my faith in the Tibetan tradition remained strong. After three years study in Dharamsala, I went to Switzerland with my teacher Geshé Rabten to further my studies of Buddhist philosophy and debate. Being in a European culture stimulated an interest in Western philosophy, psychology, and theology. I became intrigued by the existentialists, in particular by the ways in which existentialist concepts were used to understand religious experience. What motivated much of this interest was my desire to find someone who spoke in a language that would clarify my experience on the mountainside in Dharamsala. It was with great joy that I came across the Jewish philosopher Martin Buber. A passage in his book *I and Thou* struck to the core of what I had experienced:

> *The world which appears to you in this way is unreliable, for it appears always new to you, and you cannot take it by its word. It lacks density, for everything in it permeates everything else. It lacks duration, for it comes even when not called and vanishes even when you cling to it. It cannot be surveyed: if you try to make it surveyable, you lose it. It comes—comes to fetch you—and if it does not reach you or encounter you it vanishes, but it comes again transformed. It does not stand outside you, it touches your ground. It does not help you to survive; it only helps you to have intimations of eternity.*[3]

It was not until I delved into the Chinese tradition that I began to find passages from Buddhist texts—Zen and Hua Yen—that had the same resonance.

These extracurricular studies began to absorb me more than much of what I was studying with Geshé Rabten. I found myself in a position once again where I was simultaneously both inside and outside the Tibetan tradition—not a very comfortable position to be in. Inevitably it gave rise to further doubts about the claims of the Tibetans. For I had naively started this course in logic and debate through heeding the claims of the lamas that reason alone could prove the truth of many Buddhist axioms: the infallibility of the Buddha, rebirth, emptiness, and so on.

What I realized in the end was that, despite all the claims, reason was subordinate to faith. In other words: *you only set out to prove what you have already decided to believe.* As a Westerner I had assumed, wrongly it turned out, that the Tibetans saw logic as I had been taught to see it: as a Socratic enquiry where you subject propositions to ruthless analysis in order to discover whether they are true or false. The Tibetan Buddhist approach (like that of the medieval schoolmen in Europe with regard to Christianity) is to analyze a point of Buddhist doctrine in order to prove that it is true (or to analyze a point of non-Buddhist or inferior Buddhist doctrine to prove that it is false). If the logic starts weakening, as in the "proof" of previous lives, for example, then that's too bad for the logic.

There were now three factors conspiring against my commitment to Tibetan Buddhism: the insights derived from my practice of mindfulness, my experience in Dharamsala, and my critical views developed out of my studies of existentialism and Western philosophy. Persevering with my Tibetan studies and practices in this context gave rise to increasing inner conflict. This led me to undergo a course of Jungian analysis in Zurich, which was extremely helpful, but also served to drive yet another wedge between myself and the Tibetans. It was out of this situation that I decided to train in Zen.

What I was looking for was a practice of formless meditation and a place to train over an extended period of time. But at that time I could not find a teacher within any of the Tibetan traditions who taught such a practice without the embellishments of guru-devotion, tantric ritual, mantra, visualization, and so on for which I felt little affinity. The Tibetan argument that such practices were necessary as a basis for proceeding into the formless meditations of *mahamudra* or *dzog-chen* were unconvincing. I only had to look at the Theravada or Zen systems to see that a formless meditation was quite happily practiced without that basis. By this time I found it quite impossible to accept the Tibetans' critique of the other traditions and their own claims to superiority. The lamas persisted in refuting only antiquated notions of the other Buddhist traditions—notions which had been preserved in Tibet for centuries—but had little understanding of the current condition of the schools they were criticizing.

I had had an attraction to Zen for years. I loved the aesthetic dimension, the paradoxes, the simplicity, the direct earthiness of the tradition. But I'd also been repelled by much of what I had learned about it from Japanese sources: the quasi-military strictness, a certain fascination with pain, and, frankly, a kind of trivialization, whereby mystical paradox was routinely reduced to affectations of speech and behavior.

Finally, I was drawn to Songgwang Sa Monastery in South Korea. A friend, on returning from a visit to the Far East, lent me a book called *Nine Mountains* by Kusan Sunim, the resident Zen master at Songgwang Sa. Although I found much of this book incomprehensible, it introduced me to the highly appealing idea of the cultivation of doubt as a meditative practice.

As far as I know, none of the Indian Buddhist traditions, either Theravadin or Tibetan, have developed the notion of "doubt" in the sense it has acquired in Zen. The Chinese adage: "Great doubt: great enlightenment / Little doubt: little enlightenment / No doubt: no enlightenment" would make little sense for most traditional Tibetan lamas or Theravadin *acharyas*. Although the *Discourse to the Kalamas* reminds us of the value of doubt, the Indian tradition has not developed the theme of doubt any further.

For the Indo-Tibetan schools of Buddhism doubt is understood as something primarily negative. This understanding is reinforced by two traditions: those of Dharmakirti and the *Abhidharma*. In Dharmakirti's cognitive psychology, doubt is defined as a mental factor that vacillates between two alternatives. It is uncertainty, indecision. Its sole virtue is that it serves as a kind of hinge that allows invalid knowledge to swing over towards valid knowledge. For example, the thought "I doubt that all things are impermanent but perhaps they are" can swing over to "Everything probably is impermanent but I'm still not entirely sure." Such doubt is then resolved through belief ("I'm convinced that all things are impermanent"), which acts as the necessary basis for *pramana:* an authoritative cognition of what is actually the case.

In the *Abhidharma* systems of all the Indian-based schools, doubt is treated as a *klesha,* a disturbing psychological factor that clouds the clarity of mind and prevents progress along the path. The Theravadins consider doubt as one of the five main hindrances to meditation practice. Neither the *Abhidharma* nor the *Pramana* traditions encourage a positive conception of doubt as found in Zen.

Now listen to this account of doubt given by the 17th-century Japanese Zen master Takasui: "You must doubt deeply, again and again, asking yourself what the subject of hearing could be. Pay no attention to the various illusory thoughts and ideas that may occur to you. Only doubt more and more deeply, gathering together in yourself all the strength that is in you, without aiming at anything or expecting anything in advance, without intending to be enlightened and without even intending not to be enlightened; become like a child within your own breast."[4] This is "great doubt," so-called, according to Keiji Nishitani, because it refers to "the consciousness of our mode of being and way of existing in response to the great matter of birth and death."[5]

Such doubt is neither a cognitive hinge, nor a psychological defect, but a state of existential perplexity. It is not resolved through adopting a set of beliefs and achieving a pseudo-certainty, but deliberately intensified, or "coagulated" as the texts say, into a "mass of doubt." In other words, the deepest doubts or questions you have about existence are realized to be the key which, if turned correctly and with the right force, can open the door to their "response." This existential perplexity is the very place within us where awakening is the closest. To deny it and adopt a comforting set of beliefs is to renounce the very impulse that keeps one on track.

Doubt is central to the spiritual crisis many people find themselves in today. The beliefs of traditional religion having been undermined, it is often doubt we experience as the core of our spiritual awareness. Such doubt is not merely uncertainty about the claims of a particular spiritual tradition, but doubt about what is the meaning of our existence in this world. It is precisely this kind of doubt that Zen takes up and channels towards awakening. In this sense, the Zen path of doubt has a tantric dimension. Just as in India and Tibet desire and other *kleshas* were transformed into the path, so in Zen doubt is transformed into the path. The energetic power of what is conventionally conceived as an obstacle, a defilement or delusion, is thus used as a vehicle for freedom and illumination.

The Zen tradition often speaks of three factors that need to be cultivated along the path: great faith, great doubt, and great courage. Thus faith and doubt are brought together. Clearly, doubt in this context does not refer to the kind of wavering indecision in which we get stuck, preventing any positive movement. It means to keep alive the perplexity at the heart of our life, to acknowledge that fundamentally we do not know what is going on, to question whatever arises within us. The acceptance of such doubt as basic to Buddhist practice qualifies the meaning of faith. Faith is not equivalent to mere belief. Faith is the condition of ultimate confidence that we have the capacity to follow the path of doubt to its end. And courage: courage is the strength needed to be true to ourselves under all conditions, to cast aside the obstacles that are constantly thrown in our way.

3

What Is It?

I spent much of my first day in Korea lying on a warm stone floor covered with smooth yellow-ochre paper in a small room illuminated by whatever light could filter through the rice paper pasted to the latticed doors and windows. I listened to the rain pouring down upon the heavy tiled roofs, the tread of bare feet walking along the wooden walkway around the building, and the splashing of water in the muddy courtyard.

I was awakened the following morning at three by the sound of a heavy wooden-fish being struck by a monk circumambulating the courtyard. He began to accompany this thudding beat with the fervent recitation of a sutra. Together, these lonely, plaintive sounds drifted through the still night air, becoming louder as he approached and fading as he walked away. After several minutes, a number of metallic chimes were sounded. These were followed by the rapid striking of a large wooden-fish with a pair of drumsticks. Then, softly at first, the thunderous echoing rhythms of the main drum spread across the monastery of Songgwang Sa in relentless waves. At last they ceased, and there was silence again. But the next moment this quiet was shattered by the deep resonating note of the main bell as it was pounded with the full force of a heavy log. Just as the final reverberating tones died away, it was struck again. And again twenty or thirty more times, until a smaller gong interrupted from the Buddha hall to call the monks to their morning service.

"WHAT IS IT? GREAT DOUBT—
THEN CERTAINLY GREAT AWAKENING."
MT. CHOGYE. STONE LION. CALLIGRAPHY BY KUSAN SUNIM.

I breakfasted uneasily, not sure yet of how to use the four bowls on the floor in front of me. Nor was I accustomed to seaweed, pickled cabbage, and stodgy rice at six in the morning. And this unease was compounded by the imminent prospect of my first interview with Kusan Sunim, about whom I knew little, even though I had travelled halfway round the world to meet him.

Kusan Sunim's quarters were located in a small compound at the rear of the monastery adjoining an imposing lecture room and meditation hall. This area was slightly elevated on the hillside and from here I looked out over the main courtyard around which stood all the halls, shrines, and other buildings of the monastery. Accompanied by a translator, I entered the Zen master's room and bowed three times on the floor. He was a tiny, radiant man of about seventy with a shining, freshly shaven head. He smiled with much kindness but I sensed a glint of anarchy in his eyes. He was dressed in loose gray cotton clothing and sat crosslegged behind a low, gnarled table which had been painstakingly carved from the base of a large tree. He listened with patient bemusement as I nervously explained why I had come to Korea and expressed my wish to study with him. He confidently told me just to look into the nature of my mind and ask myself "What is it?"

My arrival in the country had been rushed. I had barely accustomed myself to the routines of the monastery before the three-month summer meditation retreat began. A confusing succession of bells rang out, summoning the forty or so monks who had assembled at Songgwang Sa that season to the lecture hall for the formal opening of the retreat.

Kusan Sunim pounded his heavy wooden staff on the platform and asked, "Is your original face brilliantly clear to you?"

No one said a word.

He insisted, "If you have the Dharma-eye, say something!"
Again there was silence.

He gave a loud shout, "HAK!" and said, 'When the eye
on the boulder opens, then you will understand."

He read a verse he had composed:

In the beginning awakening shines perfectly.
Now the circle of illumination is scattered with broken tiles
Which people claim are precious gems.
Flowers bob softly on the river as they float beneath the bridge.

He turned to his audience with an impish smile and casu-
ally asked what kind of teaching these swallows could be
giving. After another perplexed silence he replied for us,
"Brrr, skwok, skwok, brrr . . ."

There then followed a more intelligible account of Zen
practice, "The Dharma taught by the Buddhas and patriarchs is medicine prescribed according to the kind of disease.
What would be the use of medicine if there were no disease
to fight? The darkness of the mind is due to your delusive
thoughts and emotions alone. When you find yourselves
in good or bad circumstances, you neglect your true mind
and surrender to the power of conditions. To be swayed by
circumstance and to indulge in rash, ill-considered actions
causes the mind to be diseased. For the great truth to
appear, stop all this now. Throw it away! To awaken your
mind, press your face against the wall and ask with all your
strength, 'What is it?'"

The retreat began in earnest the following morning at
two. And this insane routine—thirteen hours of meditation ending at ten at night—was to continue for eighty-nine

more days. Fifty minutes seated on a cushion followed by ten minutes walking briskly round the hall, each session measured by the tedious ticking of an ancient clock and the shocking cracks of a wooden clapper: such were the new parameters of my temporal world, interrupted only for food (as above) and insufficient sleep.

The first two weeks were the worst. After that knees and mind become resigned and, imperceptibly, the routine switches from an outrageous exception to the very norm against which all else is understood.

The hall is bare, without windows. The lattice doors are pasted over with rice paper, allowing only degrees of sunlight to enter from outside. I spend ages examining the tiniest defects in the application of the wallpaper: a rip here, a wrinkle there. I know intimately the mottles of the square of waxed ochre-paper on the floor below me. As I walk around the room in silent procession with the seven other gray-clad figures, my feet await the flagstone that rocks slightly if trodden on at precisely the right point. Without fail, I notice the rusting smear of blood on one wall where a mosquito met its end.

The detail of the altar is too profuse to be of much interest. Set inside a wall, sealed behind glass, is a statue of Manjushri. But I am more drawn to a small cloth bag, covered in dust, that hangs above the bodhisattva's shoulder. Beneath the statue a wooden shelf supports two candlesticks, a bowl for water, and a censer filled with sand. Twice a day, before the early-morning and evening sittings, we dress in our gray butterfly-sleeved gowns and brown formal robes and bow three times in the direction of these objects.

As the water is thrown outside, the burning tip of the incense stifled in the sand, and the candles snuffed out, we refold the gowns and robes and place them over the bamboo pole that hangs suspended by rope from the ceiling.

Apart from the brief daily cleaning, this is all that "happens" in the hall. The rest of the time I am expected to "ask with all my strength, 'What is it?'" Or "What is this?" or simply "What?" Perhaps "Why is it?" or "Why is this?" I am told that it is the questioning, the doubt, that matters, not the words.

Larger spans of time are measured in fortnights by the waxing and waning of the moon. New moon and full moon signal a day off—in effect half a day off, since the early morning and evening sessions (the toughest ones naturally) are unaffected. On these days we shave each others' heads and wallow naked in a great tub of hot water. For lunch something special is prepared: "sticky" rice with chestnuts and dried persimmons, or burdock root, or *naengmyon*— cold noodles that resemble bundles of elastic bands. The empty afternoon stretches dreamily before me; time unbroken by clocks and clappers slips away like water.

Each morning in the dining hall another yesterday is torn from the calendar and thrown away. But as I look back I encounter only an abyss of vanished moments. For no landmarks stand out to separate one day from the next; nothing by which we measure the passing of time has taken place. It is in the nature of retreats that any interruption to routine be banished.

"Bath-day" is followed by "lecture-day." In the morning we gather to listen to the Vinaya Master recite the monastic vows. And in the afternoon Kusan Sunim gives another of his half-obscure and half-admonitory talks. Afterwards we foreigners troop up to his room for tea and questions. The jovial atmosphere does not mean that much is ever resolved. The parting words are much the same each time, "Since you do not understand, you must return to your cushion and ask, 'What is it?'"

And so the moon swells and vanishes for three months while a small group of humans sit cross-legged on cushions struggling with an impossible question. By the midway point, it becomes hard to believe that I ever did anything else. Memories are just more of the same inner telex, clattering away to little effect. But as the tantalizing end of the retreat peeks over the horizon and draws nearer each day, restlessness begins to eat at you: plans are pulled out from the lockers of the subconscious and dusted off; bus schedules are contemplated; maybe a movie in the local town . . . The last week is probably worse than the first.

Then it's all over. The next retreat doesn't start until December. That's three months to go with nothing to do. Choices to make: but where do I begin? The trip into town was not as enjoyable as I had made it out to be; long weeks of immobility make you prone to be sick on buses. It's a relief to return to Songgwang Sa. In a few days, the monastery settles into a slower, less pressured routine. I use the time to write: to catch up with correspondence, make notes, jot down ideas; perhaps I'll do some research, write some essays. There's time to read as well, and discuss with the others what has happened for them. I find myself trying to make sense of it all, groping yet again for words and meanings. Still at the root of it lies the question, "What is this?" Not so much as words any more, rather as the perplexity of being alive.

One of the first things I wanted to know was how this method of radical questioning developed in the Chinese Zen tradition. I discovered some of the earliest instances quoted from a text called *Records of the Masters and Disciples of the Lankavatara,* written between 713 and 716 by a Chinese monk called Ching Chüeh. The first example concerned Gunabhadra (394–468), who was connected with the Zen tradition only indirectly on account of his being the translator of the *Lankavatara Sutra,* a key text of early Zen, into Chinese. It recounted, "When [Gunabhadra] was imparting wisdom to others, before he had even begun to preach the Dharma, he would assess . . . things by pointing at a leaf and [asking], 'What is that?'"[1]

In the same text the first Zen patriarch, Bodhidharma, is likewise recorded as having employed this method in his teaching, "The Great Master [Bodhidharma] also pointed at things and inquired of their meaning, simply pointing at a thing and calling, 'What is that?' He asked about a number of things, switching their names about and asking about them [again] differently."[2]

Ching Chüeh also finds an instance of such direct questioning in the teachings of the fifth patriarch of the Zen school, Hung Jen. The Great Master [Hung Jen] said, "'There is a single little house filled with crap and weeds and dirt—what is it?' He also said, 'If you sweep out all the crap and weeds and dirt and clean it all up so there is not a single thing left inside, then what is it?'"[3]

From Hung Jen's disciple Hui Neng, the supposedly illiterate peasant who rose to become the sixth patriarch, we can trace a continuity of this kind of questioning which leads us right up to the present day. Contemporary teachers in Korea will usually point to the following encounter between Huai Jang and Hui Neng as the starting point for their tradition.

Sometime around the turn of the eighth century Huai Jang, then a young monk in his twenties, journeyed on foot to Mt. Ts'ao Ch'i in Southern China to see Hui Neng. Upon arriving at the monastery, the patriarch asked where he had just come from. Huai Jang replied that he had come from Mt. Sung, where he had visited another Zen teacher called Hui An.

Hui Neng then surprised him by asking, "What is this thing and how did it get here?"

Huai Jang was speechless. Eight years later, though, he was suddenly awakened, and said to the patriarch, "I have experienced some awakening."

The patriarch asked, "What is it?"

Huai Jang replied, "To say it is like something is not to the point."

"Can it still be cultivated and experienced?" asked Hui Neng.

Huai Jang replied, "Although its cultivation and experiencing are not uncalled for, it cannot be tainted."

The patriarch said, "Just that which cannot be tainted is protected and thought of by all Buddhas. It is so for you and also for me."[4]

Very little else is recorded about the life and teachings of Huai Jang. It is said that he served Hui Neng for fifteen

A Genealogy of the Masters
T'ang Dynasty China, 618–907

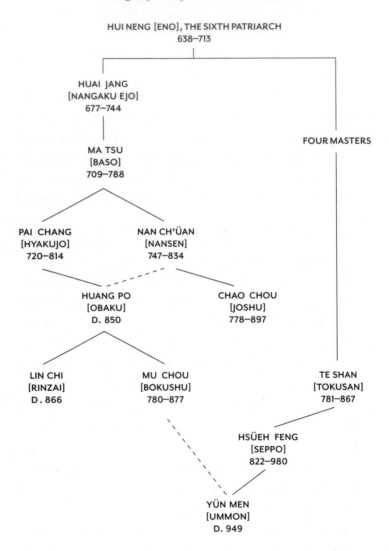

HUI NENG [ENO], THE SIXTH PATRIARCH
638–713

HUAI JANG
[NANGAKU EJO]
677–744

FOUR MASTERS

MA TSU
[BASO]
709–788

PAI CHANG
[HYAKUJO]
720–814

NAN CH'ÜAN
[NANSEN]
747–834

HUANG PO
[OBAKU]
D. 850

CHAO CHOU
[JOSHU]
778–897

LIN CHI
[RINZAI]
D. 866

MU CHOU
[BOKUSHU]
780–877

TE SHAN
[TOKUSAN]
781–867

HSÜEH FENG
[SEPPO]
822–980

YÜN MEN
[UMMON]
D. 949

years and then retired to a monastery on Mt. Nan Yüeh. He had six eminent disciples, the foremost of whom was the notable Ma Tsu. Ma Tsu lived and studied with Huai Jang for ten years. While Huai Jang was still alive, he formed his own community and took on the responsibility of teaching Zen.

In order to test the extent and depth of Ma Tsu's understanding, Huai Jang sent another of his disciples to visit him with the following instruction, "Wait until Ma Tsu has gone up to the Zen hall, then ask him this question, 'What is it?' Report back what he says."

The monk carried out Huai Jang's instruction and then returned to tell him, "Ma Tsu said, 'For the thirty years since my last shock, I have been short of neither salt nor sauce.'"

Huai Jang praised Ma Tsu's understanding.[5]

Ma Tsu was the only one of Huai Jang's disciples to "receive his mind." He eventually became one of the greatest Zen patriarchs. The teaching for which he is best known is that of his repeated insistence upon the identity between mind and Buddha. "All of you should realize that your own mind is Buddha, that is, this mind is Buddha's mind . . . Those who seek for the truth should realize that there is nothing to seek. There is no Buddha but mind; there is no mind but Buddha."[6]

Upon being asked by a monk why he so strongly maintained that mind is Buddha, Ma Tsu retorted, "Because I want to stop the crying of the baby."

The monk persisted, "When the crying has stopped, what is it then?"

"Not mind, not Buddha," replied Ma Tsu.[7]

The two best-known disciples of Ma Tsu were Nan Ch'üan and Pai Chang. In the opening passages of both their records we find them confronted by Ma Tsu in the dining hall. In the biography of Nan Ch'üan we read, "One day while Nan Ch'üan was serving rice gruel to his fellow monks, Ma Tsu asked him, 'What is in the wooden bucket?'"

"'Shut up, old man! You shouldn't talk about such things,'" answered Nan Ch'üan.

The rest of the monks who were studying with him did not dare to raise any questions about the exchange.[8]

And the following episode is recorded about Pai Chang: "Every time a patron sent food for the meal, as soon as Pai Chang opened up the lid of the container, Ma Tsu would lift up a cake, show it to the assembly, and say, 'What is it?' So it was every day."[9]

Pai Chang's first awakening came after he had been studying with Ma Tsu for three years. One day as he was walking along the road accompanying Ma Tsu, he heard the call of a wild duck.

Ma Tsu said, "What is that?"

Pai Chang said, "A wild duck."

After a pause, Ma Tsu asked, "Where has it gone?"

Pai Chang replied, "It's flown away."

Ma Tsu turned around, grabbed Pai Chang's nose and pulled it.

Pai Chang uttered a cry of pain.

Ma Tsu said, "When has it ever flown away?"

At these words Pai Chang had insight.[10]

Pai Chang was also a highly regarded Zen teacher of whom many sayings and stories have been passed down.

He too would use the same device that his predecessors had applied to penetrate the minds of his students: "Once when Pai Chang had finished talking about the Way and the crowd was leaving the hall, he called to them; when the people turned their heads, he said, 'What is it?'"[11]

Pai Chang's principal successor was the remarkable monk Huang Po. Reputed to have been seven foot tall with a swelling in the middle of his forehead which resembled a pearl, Huang Po lived and studied in the communities of both Pai Chang and Nan Ch'üan. Referring perhaps to his own physical appearance, he once said, "Suppose a warrior, forgetting that he was already wearing his pearl on his forehead, were to seek for it elsewhere, he could travel the whole world without ever finding it. But if someone who knew what was wrong were to point it out to him, the warrior would immediately realize that the pearl had been there all the time. So, if you students of the Way are mistaken about your own real mind, not recognizing that it is Buddha, you will consequently look for him elsewhere . . . But even after eons of diligent searching, you will not be able to attain to the Way."[12]

Elsewhere Huang Po tells us, "When, at last, in a single flash, you attain to full realization, you will only be realizing the Buddha-nature which has been with you all the time; and by all the foregoing stages you will have added nothing to it at all. You will come to look upon those eons of work and achievement as no better than unreal actions performed in a dream.[13] Your true nature is something never lost to you even in moments of delusion, nor is it gained at the moment of enlightenment."[14]

Huang Po's most famous disciple was Lin Chi ("Rinzai" as he is known in Japanese), the founder of the Lin Chi tradition of Zen. This is the tradition in which Korean Zen teachers trace back their lineages via the fourteenth century master Taego, who travelled to China and received transmission from an eighteenth generation successor of Lin Chi.

Lin Chi's approach was fierce and uncompromising, as the following well-known encounter shows:

"In this clump of raw flesh there is a true person of no status continually entering and leaving your senses. Those of you who have not yet recognized him, Look! Look!"

Then a monk came forward and asked, "What is the true person of no status?"

Coming down from his seat, Lin Chi grabbed the monk and exclaimed, "Speak! Speak!"

The monk hesitated.

Lin Chi pushed him away saying, "The true person of no status, what a dried up piece of shit he is!" Then he returned to his chamber.[15]

In addition to Lin Chi, Huang Po had another important disciple called Mu Chou. Mu Chou was a very reclusive figure who refused to reveal himself in public. He had the peculiar habit of making straw sandals and secretly putting them out on the road for the use of passing travellers. He was especially renowned for his immediate and incisive responses to questions. Once, while having tea with a scholar-monk he remarked, "I cannot save you."

The monk said, "I don't understand. Please explain, Master."

Mu Chou picked up a cake, showed it to him and asked, "What is it?"

The monk said, "A material object."

Mu Chou said, "You are the kind of fellow who should be boiled alive."[16]

Mu Chou was also the first teacher of Yün Men. Only on Yün Men's third attempt to gain admittance to Mu Chou's quarters did he succeed. As soon as he knocked on Mu Chou's door, Mu Chou said, "Who's there?"

Yün Men answered, "Me, Yün Men."

As soon as Mu Chou opened the door a little, Yün Men immediately bounded in; Mu Chou held him fast and said, "Speak! Speak!"

Yün Men hesitated, and was pushed out; he still had one foot inside when Mu Chou slammed the door, trapping Yün Men's leg. As Yün Men cried out in pain, he was suddenly greatly enlightened.[17]

Later, Mu Chou encouraged Yün Men to leave him and continue his training under another teacher, Hsüeh Feng. According to the *Blue Cliff Record*, Hsüeh Feng "talked no more of mystery or marvel nor did he speak of mind or nature. He appeared strikingly alone, like a great fiery mass; approach him and he burned off your face."[18]

Once, when Hsüeh Feng was living alone in a hut, two monks came to pay their respects to him. Seeing them coming, Hsüeh Feng pushed open the door of the hut with his hand, popped out, and said, "What is it ?"

In response the monks just said, "What is it?"

Hsüeh Feng lowered his head and went back inside the hut.[19]

On another occasion Hsüeh Feng employed this same tactic to test another disciple. As the disciple entered his room, Hsüeh Feng asked, "What is it?"

The disciple replied, "Today the weather is clear, good for asking everyone to work."[20]

It is said that after this the disciple's replies "were never out of accord with the mysterious meaning."[21]

When Yün Men arrived at Hsüeh Feng's monastery, the first thing he asked was, "What is the Buddha?"

Hsüeh Feng replied, "Don't talk in your sleep."[22]

Yün Men then bowed to him and stayed in his community for three years. Although he came to be considered as one of Hsüeh Feng's foremost successors, little seems to have been recorded of their encounters. Yün Men himself became a renowned teacher, producing more than sixty awakened disciples. He has been described as one who "was not the same as others. Sometimes he held still and stood like a wall ten miles high, with no place for you to draw near. Sometimes he would open out a path for you, die along with you and live along with you."[23]

Yün Men had a disciple called Hsiang Lin who served as his attendant for eighteen years. Throughout this time Yün Men would often just call out to him, "Attendant!" As soon as he responded, Yün Men would say, "What is it?" At such times, no matter how much Hsiang Lin spoke to present his understanding and gave play to his spirit, he never reached mutual accord with Yün Men.

One day, though, he suddenly said, "I understand." Yün Men said, "Why don't you say something above and beyond that?"

Hsiang Lin stayed on another three years.[24]

Yün Men died in 949, two hundred fifty years after Huai Jang went to see Hui Neng. He was acknowledged as the founder of the Yün Men tradition of Zen, one of the five major "houses" of Chinese Zen, which survived for three hundred years after his death. The twelfth century Chinese Zen master Ta Hui summed up Yün Men's elusive and penetrating teaching by citing the following remarks of his: "When you can't speak, it's there; when you don't speak, it's not there. When you can't discuss it, it's there; when you don't discuss it, it's not there . . . You tell me, what is it when you're not discussing it? . . . What else is it?"[25]

Questioning

It is most uncanny that we are able to ask questions; for to
question means to acknowledge that we do not know something. But it is more than an acknowledgment: it includes a
yearning to confront an unknown and illuminate it through
understanding. Questioning is a quest: it takes the first step
into the dark and proceeds to build a path from ignorance
to clarity, from bewilderment to recognition, from estrange-
ment to intimacy. It creates the initial fissure in the veil of
the unknown. It forms an opening through which the light
of wisdom is able to shine and penetrate. Questioning simultaneously reveals our limitations and our urge to go beyond
them.

Calculation

There are two distinct kinds of questioning. The most common type is that which solves the problems which occur in
daily life. If something fails to work in the way we expect it
to, we ask ourselves why and begin to search for the causes
and reasons for the failure. If we come across something we
have never encountered before, we become baffled and ask

ourselves what's going on. Such questioning is one of curiosity. We are usually confident that an answer lies within
our reach: it is just a matter of figuring it out. We can apply
whatever practical skills we have learned, as well as the
powers of our own reason and memory, and rely upon the
ever-growing quantity of knowledge that has been collected
and stored by others.

Such questioning leads along a calculated path. We determine what possibilities lie ahead of us. We infer what is of
greater probability. We eliminate certain choices through
trial and error or by simple deduction. With each completed
step we calculate our next move until, finally, the problem
is solved and our curiosity is replaced with the satisfaction
of knowing.

This calculative approach has become increasingly predominant in this present century. The advances in scientific
research and technology have been made possible through
perfecting the means of calculation and, its applications.
As our world becomes ever more dominated by technical
achievements, and as we become more and more dependent
upon them, the greater is the role that a calculative attitude
comes to play in our lives.

Yet there exists another way of questioning and thinking.
Heidegger neatly summed this up in an address he gave in
1955: "Calculative thinking computes. It computes ever new,
ever more promising and at the same time more economical
possibilities. Calculative thinking races from one prospect
to the next. Calculative thinking never stops, never collects
itself. Calculative thinking is not meditative thinking, not

thinking which contemplates the meaning that reigns in everything there is."[1]

People regard a meditative attitude to life as remote, as out of touch with "real" concerns. It belongs to the province of the mystic and the philosopher. No matter how profound it may seem to be, it has no influence on the course of actual events. The fact that meditation is often viewed critically or even cynically only further indicates the degree to which a calculative attitude holds sway in people's minds today and forms their standards of evaluation. But as this world of ours, now frantically driven by the daemon of computation, uproots itself from spiritual values and hurtles into an ever more perilous future, may not it be time to consider more closely how our attitudes affect the way our life unfolds?

A calculative attitude tends to be manipulative. It treats life as though it were composed of a virtually infinite number of separate parts. This attitude not only operates in the material realm; it affects our vision of other people and even ourselves. It fragments and divides; it turns living creatures into things. To be able to calculate effectively, we must be able to measure our objects with the exactness and precision demanded by the final aim of successfully manipulating them. To control the diverse elements of reality requires that we see them as separate units capable of being dissected and accumulated, of being rejected and attained.

The ability to calculate accurately is not harmful in itself. It distorts and deludes only when its importance becomes so exaggerated that, instead of being merely one faculty among others, it casts its shadow over nearly all areas of human activity. As long as calculation is kept in its place, it can serve as a useful tool with which to accomplish many practical tasks. But it is decidedly dangerous when it becomes our predominant attitude towards life as a whole. If our view of the future as well as our ethical decisions are determined only by a calculative attitude, then we are truly in danger of losing altogether our uncertain hold on the threads of a calmer, more contemplative relationship to life.

A calculative attitude can serve us in our dealings with the practical concerns of the everyday, but can only mislead us if we apply its methods to unravel the deeper riddles of life. Calculation can solve our problems but is helpless in penetrating our mysteries. When confronting the mysterious we cannot rely upon any logical or technical means to gain insight. For as soon as we attempt to "figure out" a mystery, it ceases to be such and becomes a mere problem.[2] The more pervasive is calculation in our lives, the more is the mysterious banished. And as the sense of life's mystery becomes dimmer and more remote, so our ability to meditate diminishes—to the point where meditation is exiled to the very margins of existence.

But the mysterious lies at the heart of our lives, not at the periphery. And its presence is only felt to the extent that a meditative attitude still lives within us. Unlike a problem, a mystery can never be solved. A mystery can only be penetrated. A problem once solved ceases to be a problem; but the penetration of a mystery does not make it any less mysterious. The more intimate one is with a mystery, the greater shines the aura of its secret. The intensification of a mystery leads not to frustration (as does the increasing of a problem) but to release.

A Meditative Attitude

Meditation is widely perceived as a kind of specialized activity. It is regarded as a means of calming and concentrating the mind, as a panacea for anxiety, agitation, and tension. Symptomatic of the prevailing obsession with calculation, it is considered as a *technique,* as a systematic application of a preconceived series of ideas. But although guidelines can be given, ultimately there is no "how" to meditation. Certain exercises and skills may be more conducive to meditation than others, but in the end a meditative attitude is not something we can ever acquire.

A meditative attitude is nothing new or alien. It dwells deeply within us all; except now it is a field which increasingly lies fallow and ignored.[3] It is not something that we have to bring from elsewhere and introduce into our lives. It is already present in an embryonic and sporadic way. It may come to us unexpectedly in glimmers and hints. It is vaguely recognized as a distant, barely known possibility, which may nag at us like the fragments of a dream that refuse to be recollected yet refuse to leave us alone. We need to recognize this fragile attitude and then care for it and nurture it as we would a child or a seedling.

Meditation does not add anything to life; it recovers what has been lost. It is a growing awareness of what our existence is saying to and asking of us. It is something fundamental that has become obscured by our infatuation with a separate ego and its endless calculations and melodramas. The practice of meditation is to allow this attitude to shine through, to acquaint ourselves, both slowly and abruptly, with what is both our origin and culmination.

Meditation and mystery are inseparable. Just as the mysterious cannot be unravelled through calculation, nor can a meditative attitude be acquired as though it were a technical skill. Heidegger remarked, "That which shows itself and at the same time withdraws is the essential trait of the mystery."[4] Meditation occurs whenever our innermost awareness is trained upon the shocking nearness yet elusive distance of what is present.

The practice of meditation is a process of attrition. The mind has a seemingly infinite capacity for chatter. And there is no instant or easy cure for this proliferation of thoughts and emotions. Only the patient continuity of meditation, what the Chinese master Hsü Yün called "a long, enduring mind,"[5] can finally wear it down. This process is echoed in Lao Tsu's words: "What is of all things most yielding can overwhelm that which is of all things most hard."[6] Water is that which is most yielding; rock that which is most hard. The patient, unhurried yet continuous flow of water can wear down even the most resistant and stubborn rock.

Meditation is closer to the valleys than the peaks. A meditative attitude is not preoccupied with peak experiences, those exhilarating heights of spiritual experience that leave the valleys and plains far below. Like water "it is content with the places that all men disdain."[7] The rarified and brilliant atmosphere of the peaks may uplift and inspire us, but we cannot live there long. Living things do not grow on the peaks; they need the fertile soil of the valley. For meditation to be fertile it too needs to stay close to the ground, to follow the humble paths along the valleys amidst the myriad details of daily life.

A meditative attitude is a creative attitude. Merely to master the techniques of painting is insufficient to create a work of art. The work of art, whether a painting, a poem, or a piece of music, needs more than mere technical mastery. Likewise, proficiency in the techniques of meditation alone is incapable of creating insight. Insight, wisdom, compassion, and love all come from a source other than that of technical mastery. The meditator is akin to an artist: proficient in his craft, an adept in creating love and wisdom.

Unknowing, Waiting, and Listening

The core of a meditative attitude is questioning itself. Such questioning, though, has nothing to do with the curiosity of calculation. Meditative questioning enquires into no individually discernable detail of life, but into the whole. The mystery of life is something in which we are inextricably involved. In contrast to a calculating enquiry, in which the inquirer is separate from the problem, only a conceptual distinction can be made between the meditator and the mystery. For meditative questioning partakes in the nature of the mystery itself. It is a kind of fundamental astonishment or perplexity reflecting that which simultaneously shows itself and withdraws.

In *Being and Having: An Existentialist Diary,* the French

philosopher and artist Gabriel Marcel remarks, "A problem is something which I meet, which I find complete before me, but which I can therefore lay siege to and reduce. But a mystery is something in which I am myself involved, and it can therefore only be thought of as a *sphere where the distinction between what is in me and what is before me loses its meaning and initial validity.* A genuine problem is subject to an appropriate technique by the exercise of which it is defined: whereas a mystery, by definition, transcends every conceivable technique.[8]

The consequence of this distinction is asserted by the Zen maxim:

> *Great doubt: great awakening.*
> *Little doubt: little awakening.*
> *No doubt: no awakening*[9]

These terse lines express how penetration of the mysterious is directly related to the degree and intensity of questioning. Doubt or questioning is seen as the indispensable key to awakening. It is the vitality of a meditative attitude, the driving force which heightens the sense of the mysterious to the point where it unexpectedly reveals what until then had remained withdrawn and unsuspected.

There is a kind of *unknowing* present in meditative questioning which is quite different from that found in the Buddhist idea of ignorance. The notion of ignorance encompasses not merely an absence of knowledge about something but also a distortion of it. In ignorance things appear in a way in which they do not exist. There is also a clinging and grasping involved which solidifies the distortion and sets it up as something real and secure. Meditative unknowing is free from such grasping and distortion. Instead of clinging, it lets go. Instead of insisting that things exist in a certain way, it accepts their mysteriousness. Such unknowing loosens our hold on the immutability of the familiar. It is simple and relaxed; it retains a naive, childlike openness.

This unknowing can be compared to the Zen concepts of "no-mind" or "no-thought," which Hui Neng defined as "to be unstained in all environments."[10] A modern Chinese Zen teacher, Garma C.C. Chang, explains, "The so-called no-mind is not like clay, wood or stone, that is, utterly devoid of consciousness; nor does the term imply that the mind stands still without any reaction when it contacts objects or circumstances in the world. It does not adhere to anything, but is natural and spontaneous at all times and under all circumstances."[11] This spontaneity and naturalness extends even to mental activity itself. "No-thought," says Hui Neng, "is not to think even when involved in thought."[12] And Ta Hui exhorts us to "be totally without knowledge and understanding, like a three-year-old child."[13]

We can arrive at this condition of unknowing in a number of ways. For some it comes as a final acceptance of the incapacity of logic and reason to cope with certain overwhelming questions. It is like the palpable silence which follows the breakdown of an apparatus which has been strained to its limits. The acknowledgment "I don't know" comes finally not as failure or disgrace but as release. In the midst of the tranquility of this newly discovered unknowing there is the intimation of a deeper and more encompassing wisdom. This unknowing is able to sense—maybe dimly at first—the stirrings of meditative awareness.

Calculation, on the other hand, refuses to submit to unknowing. The unknowing which spurs such an enquiry on to find a solution is felt as a challenge to be overcome and eliminated. Calculation prides itself on knowledge. To be successful one must be able to rely on what is known in order to dispel the unknown confronted in a problem. What is not known is regarded as both an uncomfortable lacuna in the field of knowledge as well as the indispensable stimulus for further understanding. Unknowing is the enemy of the calculative attitude, yet at the same time that which enables it to progress. Calculation, as a struggle against the unknown, is never simple or relaxed; it is incapable of ever unwinding what it has set in motion.

A meditative attitude is eternally prepared to *wait*. Freed from any pretensions of knowing, nothing in particular is expected to happen. Such waiting is content to let things be while at the same time acknowledging that, concealed within the mystery, there is an unknown. That which lies hidden cannot be coaxed forth. It has its own time beyond the time of what can be recollected and anticipated. Waiting waits; it is alert to every moment but has no expectations.[14]

Expectation is characteristic of calculation. Our calculations are only able to proceed as long as we can foresee a certain result. If we were unable to expect something from such a procedure (even if it is just the proof that our hypothesis is flawed), then we would have no incentive to undertake it. Calculation is goal-oriented; every step it makes is taken

in anticipation of some result. Expectation draws its nour-
ishment from the past. Out of all our recollections it pieces
together an image of what is desired, and then projects it
into the future as an anticipated goal. In expecting something, we devise a bridge between the past and the future
that exists only in our thoughts.

It is fatal in meditation to entertain expectations. As soon
as we fix in our mind a picture of what it is we seek to attain,
we restrict ourselves to the boundaries of the known. The
only notions we will ever be capable of producing will be
drawn from the pool of impressions, ideas, symbols, and
experiences we have stored in our memory. Even such noble
ideas as "awakening" and "Buddha" are finally nothing
but collages of past impressions stuck together by logic and
imagination. Such images can serve as signs to help guide us
along the path, but should never be allowed to intrude into
our meditative penetration of the mysterious. If they, or any
other image of a goal, attempt to foreshadow the unpredictable and unknown, then meditation will be trapped within
thought, memory, and imagination and separated from its
mystery.

One of the greatest dangers of all lies in the recollection
of our own experiences in meditation. It is not so unusual
while meditating to awaken to something extraordinary and
unprecedented. But the more unusual and mystical is the
experience, the greater will be the danger. For we will be
tempted, once the immediate experience has faded, to place
an image of it before us and then strive to recapture it. Once
this happens, and we confidently proceed under the illusion
that the unpredictable will from now on conform to our

well-founded expectations, then genuine meditative questioning is lost. Thus the beginner has a great advantage over
the experienced meditator.

With no idea or picture of what might happen, we simply have to wait. No amount of experience can predict the
ways in which the mysterious will unfold. In waiting, as
with unknowing, we cannot resort to our stores of accumulated knowledge. But in leaving them behind we enter not
a state of blank indifference, but one of vivid, unprejudiced
questioning.

If we draw an analogy with sense-consciousness, a meditative attitude *listens* rather than looks. Listening is more
receptive than looking. In attuning our ears we sharpen our
attention so that it opens up to the vast and subtle range of
sounds that constantly surround and assail us. Even when
we select and concentrate on a particular sound, we do so in
such a way that the sound is allowed greater ease of access to
enter us. Looking, however, is often characterized by a nar-
rowing of the attention and an almost acquisitive focusing
upon its object. It is not that the form of the object is being
allowed to enter consciousness; rather, it is we who seize and
invade it.[15]

Meditative awareness listens. It is receptive to whatever
occurs just as our ears are sensitive to the ever present sym-
phony of sound and silence that engulf us. In the simplicity
of waiting, why not listen for the footfall of the mysterious
than look out for a visionary sign?

The importance of listening as a symbol for wisdom is
attested to in many traditions. In the Sumerian language, for
example, the very same word is used to denote both ear and

wisdom.[16] At one point in the *Shurangama Sutra* the Buddha asks the bodhisattvas and arhats present to speak of the most effective method for realizing awakening. Avalokiteshvara replies, "As the Buddha now asks about the best means of perfection, my method, which consists in regulating the organ of hearing so as to quiet the mind for its entry into the stream of meditation leading to the state of *samadhi* and the attainment of enlightenment, is the best."[17]

In a later passage from the same discourse, the bodhisattva Manjushri explains what Avalokiteshvara meant:

When one dwells in quiescence,
Rolls of drums from ten directions
Simultaneously are heard,
So hearing is complete and perfect.
The eyes cannot pierce a screen,
And neither can mouth nor nose;
Body only feels when it is touched.
Mind's thoughts are confused and unconnected,
But sound whether near or far
At all times can be heard.
The five other organs are not perfect,
But hearing truly is pervasive.[18]

If we turn to de Saint Exupéry's *The Little Prince* we find a passage where the hero encounters a fox who, at the end of their meeting, reveals the secret that he had promised to tell: "It is only with the heart that one can see rightly; what is essential is invisible to the eye." In her psychological interpretation of *The Little Prince,* the Jungian analyst von Franz turns to a medieval work by Picinellus to explain some of the associations that may have been working on de Saint Exupéry's unconscious when he wrote the passage. Picinellus says, "The fox is a symbol of faith and foresight because a fox investigates things by his hearing, and thus also the Christian can perceive the divine mysteries only with his ears and not penetrate them with his eyes."[19]

The Public Case

Meditative questioning waits and listens in the simplicity of unknowing. Although quiet and freed from expectations and curiosity, it is alive with the tension of perplexity. Such questioning rarely occurs spontaneously. To be aware of the mystery at the heart of the ordinary is not something that can be summoned forth at will.

When Huai Jang was asked by Hui Neng what it was he had awakened to, he replied, "To say it is like something is not to the point."[20] As soon as the mysterious is stood alongside the familiar details of the world and compared with this or that thing, we immediately lose it. To lock it into concepts, to circumscribe it with adjectives, is a wishful attempt to bring it into the range of calculation. Still Hui Neng pressed Huai Jang to be more specific; he asked him whether it was something that could be cultivated and experienced. Huai Jang's reply exposed the crux of this dilemma: "Although its cultivation and experiencing are not uncalled for, it cannot be tainted." The paradox is that even though the mysterious "it" can never be influenced, manipulated, or in any way affected by what we do, it is still worthwhile to train ourselves in such a way that we are more exposed to its unpredictable nature.

An important element in this training is a method which seems to have originated with Yün Men but has been passed down to us through the descendants of Lin Chi.[21] Since awareness of the mysterious is sporadic and uncertain, the most we can do is cultivate a way of being more receptive to it. In the tradition of Lin Chi, this is achieved by recollecting one of the many accounts from the records of the past in which a sudden awakening to the mysterious is conveyed. By focusing on the critical moment of the episode, a clue is given to the extraordinary character of the mysterious itself.

The Chinese, with their combination of devotion to antiquity and a scrupulous regard for recording history, compiled many collections of anecdotes, sayings, and instructions that illustrate moments of sudden awakening. These episodes are referred to as "public cases," which is the literal meaning of the sometimes misunderstood term *kung an,* or in Japanese pronunciation, "koan."

The term "public case" was adopted from the Chinese legal vocabulary.[22] In its original sense it referred to the record of a court case which was significant enough to serve as a precedent in making future legal decisions. The lawbooks probably came to be filled with such cases. Later, the same term came to be used to describe the records of the awakenings of Zen masters.

Just as a judge studies a previous legal case to get his bearings on the complexities of a present case, so can the Zen student study a public case to get his bearings on the complexities of the present "case" of his or her own existential dilemma. The account of a previous court case will never exactly duplicate the details of the one at hand. It is incapable of providing a ready-made solution that can just be transferred to a present case. All it can offer is an orientation, an example, a sense of direction. Likewise, the unique circumstances of an awakening related in the Zen records will never be repeated. These cases do not offer an answer to our own current existential predicament; they can only provide an indication of the way ahead.

To make use of a public case in meditation, we must first become familiar with the situation depicted in the case. When this is clear, then attention can be focused on the crucial point around which the case turns. Take the case of the encounter between Huai Jang and Hui Neng. The situation described here extends over a period of years. It starts with a question; Hui Neng asks Huai Jang, "What is this thing and how did it get here?" It is resolved when, eight years later, Huai Jang suddenly awakens to what Hui Neng was talking about. To test his student's insight, Hui Neng repeats the question in it most essential form, "What is it?" Huai Jang then further articulates his understanding and Hui Neng acknowledges its validity.

In meditating on this case, it is unnecessary to dwell upon every detail. We must single out the vital point. Here this is the twice repeated question of Hui Neng, which first shocks Huai Jang into silence but subsequently provokes his insight. The concluding dialogue also gives some useful hints. But it is this forceful questioning by Hui Neng that drives the case unswerving to its resolution.

The value of this case lies in the way it shows the central role of questioning in the meditative attitude. *What is it?* There are few questions as fundamental as this. It presents the deepest question about human existence stripped of any religious or cultural embellishments. It stares the mysterious in the face, unshielded by any comforting explanations. And as the case proceeds we realize that this simple act of doubt was in itself sufficient to awaken Huai Jang's mind from its slumber. During the eight years he stayed with Hui Neng, there is no mention of his receiving any other guidance. Their spiritual relationship is summed up in the single, uncompromising question "What is it?"

A meditative attitude need not depend upon any formal method to sustain itself. In essence it moves in wordless yet vivid silence. But if that silence eludes us, then it may help to adopt methods that help us enter and remain in the vivid tranquility of meditation. Of the numerous methods taught in the Buddhist tradition, one would be to contemplate the question "What is it?" The aim of this method is to provoke a sensation of questioning or doubt. The danger, however, is that one may just repeat the question as though it were a mantra, without giving rise to a real sense of enquiry. If the question is just repeated, the mind may eventually become calm and still; but such quiescence alone is insufficient to create a true meditative attitude.[23]

Although contemplation of the question "What is it?" is usually regarded as a form of *kung an* practice associated with the Lin Chi tradition of Zen Buddhism, there is a striking interpretation of it by Dogen, the founder of the Japanese Soto Zen school. In the "Buddha-nature" section of his monumental work the *Shobogenzo,* Dogen says, "What is the essence of the World Honored One's words, 'Everything is a living being: all beings are the Buddha-nature?' They are a verbal preaching of 'What is it that thus comes?'"[24] The question "What is it that thus comes?" is the very question posed by Hui Neng to Huai Jang (translated here as "What is this thing and how did it get here?"). The contemporary Zen scholar Masao Abe offers the following explanation:

> The question, *"What* is it that *thus* comes?" that Huai Jang took eight years to solve refers to the Buddhist truth, and in Dogen's present case, to the essential point of the words, "All things are the Buddha-nature." . . . Zen often indicates the ultimate reality by interrogatives as well as by negatives such as "nothingness" and "emptiness." An interrogative "what" or "whence" is that which cannot be grasped by the hand, that which cannot be defined by the intellect; it is that which can never be objectified, that which one can never obtain, no matter what one does. Indeed, "what" or "whence" is unknowable, unnameable, unobjectifiable, and unobtainable, and therefore limitless and infinite. Since the Buddha-nature is limitless and boundless, without name, form, or color, it can be well, indeed best, expressed by such an interrogative. This is the reason Dogen finds the essence of his idea "All beings are the Buddha-nature" precisely in the question "What is it that thus comes?"[25]

The point, then, is that the question "What is it?" is not enquiring *about* anything. It is not as though the question is one thing and the meaning of reality another. Especially for the purpose of direct meditative questioning, "What is it?" simply expresses reality more adequately than such terms as "impermanence," "emptiness," "Buddha-nature" and so on. To the extent that we can express it in words, the mystery of life is best expressed as a question.

Such meditation as this starts from a standpoint of non-duality. We cannot merely aim at a state of non-duality as though it were some kind of a goal. For the essence of this questioning is the enquiry into that which does the questioning. In other words, to ask "What is it?" means to ask "What is it that asks 'What is it?'" It means that the "it" of "What is it?" is that which asks "what" or, better still, the "it" *is* the "what." In practice, this is not as convoluted as it sounds; neither is there a real problem of infinite regression. The perplexed enquiry into this mystery called life is simply part of the very mystery itself. This is a path of non-dual questioning. The mystery, in revealing itself as "What is it?" is the practice—nothing else.

The question "What is it?" is only a means to activate and sharpen the quality of meditative questioning. Once it has served this purpose and we are gripped by the sensation of doubt itself, then it is no longer necessary to use it as a formal device. It may be helpful at times to recollect the question when the sensation of doubt weakens or disappears, but it would only be an obstacle if we were to insist on retaining it once it has achieved its purpose. When the sensation of doubt has been established, it can also be of value to contemplate other public cases and consider the different shades of perplexity that they invoke.

THE HEART SUTRA

Both the form and the style of the public cases recorded in the Zen tradition have a distinctly Chinese flavor. The cases represent a mature phase in the evolution of Chinese Buddhism, in which the original doctrines, first imported from India some five hundred years before the time of Hui Neng, have become thoroughly Sinicized. Although Buddhist in their frame of reference, the public cases are as much reminiscent of the Taoist writings of Chuang Tzu as any Buddhist sutras translated from Sanskrit. In contrast to the mind-dazzling vistas of the Indian Mahayana texts, the Chinese felt more at home with simple, earthy images drawn from nature and daily life. Instead of dehistoricized Buddhas and bodhisattvas, the Zen masters appear as undeniably human figures replete with all manner of idiosyncrasies. Unfortunately, these stylistic and cultural differences have tended to conceal the universal applicability of the Zen approach to truth.

Any written or oral record describing a situation which triggered a spiritual awakening will bear many similarities with the public cases of Zen Buddhism. The value of a *kung an* lies in its potential to provoke a meditative attitude. The cultural and linguistic form through which it is expressed is of secondary importance. What reason is there to assume that the ways in which Zen has used its public cases cannot be applied to similar accounts from other traditions? The popular notion of the *kung an* as a spiritual riddle from the Far East has been largely responsible for obscuring its wider meaning. Even the Zen records themselves contain cases which are not accounts of Chinese masters but episodes from Indian Buddhist sutras.[26] The paradoxical core around which the public cases turn indicates not anything peculiarly "Zen" but simply the mystery of life itself.

Take, for example, the Indian Buddhist *Heart Sutra*.[27] As a condensation of the elaborate *Perfection of Wisdom Discourses (Prajñaparamita Sutra),* this short text is commonly recited and studied in all schools of Mahayana Buddhism. But how often has it been pointed out that it has many characteristics of a *kung an?* Typical of most Indian Buddhist writings, it gives nearly no sense of a historical setting or individual human personalities. It primarily presents an awesome metaphysical doctrine. But if we downplay these elements and summarize the sutra in a manner more compatible with a Chinese legal record, it might read something like this:

> When old Shakyamuni was staying on Vulture's Peak he encouraged his disciple Shariputra to go and visit Avalokiteshvara. Upon reaching where the bodhi-sattva lived, Shariputra asked: "What is the perfection of wisdom?" Avalokiteshvara replied, "Form is emptiness and emptiness is form." Upon hearing about this, Shakyamuni said, "Very good. Well said."

In this reading, the *Heart Sutra* is transformed into an account which would not look out of place in any collection of Zen public cases. In highlighting the interplay of the three characters and showing how the text turns around the perplexing equivalence of form and emptiness, the sutra becomes transparent to a Zen interpretation.[28] As with other koans the text records a historical moment of illumination contained within a wider situation. The crucial point of the sutra, which could serve to activate a meditative attitude of perplexity and doubt, is the statement, "Form is emptiness and emptiness is form." Although other Buddhist schools have produced rational interpretations of this famous line, the Zen approach would be to treat it as a keyhole to the mysterious.

An inevitable conflict exists between a meditative attitude and any technique of meditation. A mind that is restless and distracted, prone to bouts of torpor, depression, and worry, and above all, habituated to calculation, is incapable of more than passing moments of genuine meditation. There is no alternative but to adopt a prescribed method of meditation as a way towards a meditative attitude. Even those who are more naturally contemplative than others will probably require aids and guidelines to help sustain and deepen their meditation. This conflict between the attitude and the technique is rooted in the gulf between the meditative and the calculative, the mysterious and the problematic.

A technique of meditation is a means to achieve an end. It is usually comprised of a series of steps which pass through a series of spiritual "levels." As a technique it belongs to the domain of calculation; its failure to produce the desired result can be treated as a problem to be solved by a reassessment of one's technical competence. A meditative attitude, however, is not merely a means but actually partakes in the nature of the end.[29] It cannot be dissected into stages and levels because it is already whole and complete. It is incapable of being reduced to a technical procedure; for it belongs to the sphere of mystery and is unconcerned with the mere solving of problems.

No amount of calculating thought can solve the paradoxical cases of the Zen tradition. These public cases call for an alternative approach. They astonish and perplex: they point to a mystery, not to a problem. They are like mirrors which can reflect the untapped depths of human experience. It is futile to examine them with the conventional tools of analysis and reason. One has to look at them in an altogether different way. As you probe them and turn them, gaze at and listen to them, they may suddenly reveal a hitherto unrealized intuition of their meaning. Yet despite its meta-technical content, as soon as you select a *kung an* and train your attention to dwell on it, this procedure may quickly assume the characteristics of a technique.

Every prescribed method will, to some extent, compromise the authenticity of a meditative attitude. Given our distracted and confused condition, this is hardly surprising. Although moments of unconditioned meditation may occur with greater or lesser frequency, for longer or shorter periods of time, we are destined to a conflict between the spontaneity of the mysterious and the gradations of technique.

Fragments of a Twenty-Fifth Century Discourse on Letting Go

Editor's note: *The* Fragments *were recovered some years ago from the site of Sung-kuang-ssu, a monastery of the Ch'an tradition situated at the northeastern corner of the Korean peninsula. They were included in a bundle of loose miscellaneous papers. We attribute their authorship to a certain Fa Ch'üan on account of a personal seal marked with this name stamped to the final page. About Fa Ch'üan himself nothing is known. Since the text is written in English and some of the accompanying papers in the same hand are dated from 2524, we can suppose that Fa Ch'üan was of European or American origin. He probably belonged to the small foreign community which apparently lived in Sung-kuang-ssu from about 2520 to 2530. Usnelli has already pointed out that the* Fragments *are an early Buddhist excavation of parts of a work entitled* Gelassenheit *by the controversial twenty-fifth century thinker and prophet Martin Heidegger (2432–2519). Following the colophon of* Gelassenheit *we can conclude that this discourse was held at some time between 2487–8.*

1

Subhuti: The meaning of "letting go" is unclear to me but I suspect that it awakens when the bodhisattva's nature lets itself penetrate desirelessness.

Shariputra: Letting something go implies quiescence. But the letting go of the bodhisattva has nothing to do with powerlessly letting things arise and pass away.

Subhuti: Perhaps a higher activity is concealed in this letting go than is found in all the actions of the world and the deeds of sentient beings.

Manjushri: A higher activity which is not action *(karma).*

Shariputra: Hence genuine letting go lies beyond the distinction between action and quiescence.

2

Shariputra: What does letting go have to do with the nature of mind?

Manjushri: Nothing, if according to our habitual concepts, we conceive of the mind as conceptualization. The true nature of mind is only revealed in letting go.

Shariputra: Although I desire to do so I cannot imagine the nature of mind.

Manjushri: This is because your desire and your conceptualization prevent you.

Shariputra: What then am I to do?

Subhuti: I also ask myself this.

Manjushri: We are to do nothing but wait.

3

Manjushri: We are now close to penetrating fully into the nature of mind.

Subhuti: In that we are waiting for its nature.

Manjushri: Waiting; but never expecting. For expectation involves conceiving of something.

Subhuti: Waiting lets go of all that. Waiting never involves conceptualization. Waiting has no object.

Shariputra: But we always wait *for* something whenever we wait.

Subhuti: As soon as we conceive of what we are waiting for and make it into a thing, we are truly no longer waiting.

Manjushri: In waiting we leave what we are waiting for open.

Subhuti: Why?

Manjushri: Because waiting penetrates into openness . . .

Subhuti: . . . into the expanse of distance . . .

Manjushri: . . . in whose nearness it discovers the lingering in which it abides.

Subhuti: Openness itself is that for which we can only wait.

Shariputra: Then openness itself is the dharmadhatu . . .

Manjushri: . . . into which the bodhisattva waitingly penetrates in his meditation.

4

Manjushri: What is waiting?

Shariputra: Since waiting refers to openness and openness is the dharmadhatu, waiting must be a relation to the dharmadhatu.

Manjushri: Indeed, it is *the* relation to the dharmadhatu.

Waiting penetrates into the dharmadhatu and this interpenetration lets the dharmadhatu reign purely as it is. Waiting means to penetrate into the openness of the dharmadhatu.

5

Shariputra: Being released in this way is the first moment of letting go but it is not complete letting go.

Subhuti: How not?

Manjushri: Because genuine letting go can occur although the bodhisattva is not yet released from *samsara*.

Subhuti: If genuine letting go is the appropriate relation to the dharmadhatu and if such a relation is defined in terms of that to which it is related, then genuine letting go must repose in the dharmadhatu and receive from it the movement towards it.

Manjushri: Letting go proceeds from the dharmadhatu, because in letting go the bodhisattva dwells in the dharmadhatu by virtue of the dharmadhatu itself. In his very nature he is released into the dharmadhatu because primordially he belongs within the dharmadhatu. He belongs to it because from time immemorial he has inhered within it; again, by virtue of the dharmadhatu itself.

Subhuti: Hence waiting is grounded upon the bodhisattva's belonging to that for which he waits.

Manjushri: From the experience of waiting for the dharmadhatu to open itself, waiting is spoken of as letting go.

6

Manjushri: Does the bodhisattva not already inhere within the dharmadhatu?

Shariputra: What good is that if he does not genuinely inhere?

Subhuti: Thus he does and does not inhere.

Shariputra: Again this restless duality between is and is not.

Subhuti: He is suspended between the two.

Manjushri: But his stay in this betweenness is waiting.

Subhuti: This is the nature of letting go in which the dharmadhatu encounters the bodhisattva; here he glimpses the nature of mind as letting go.

7

Manjushri: When the bodhisattva penetrates the letting go of the dharmadhatu, he desires desirelessness.

Shariputra: Letting go is true freedom from *samsara* and the abandonment of the desire for any limits. This abandonment no longer comes from desire. But the moment the bodhisattva penetrates into the dharmadhatu requires a trace of desire. This trace, however, vanishes in the act of penetration and is fully extinguished in letting go.

8

Manjushri: Being absorbed in the letting go of the dharmadhatu is the nature of the spontaneity of mind. It is noble-mindedness itself. Thus rejoicing in waiting, the bodhisattva becomes more waitful and more empty.

Subhuti: Apparently emptier but richer in possibilities.

Shariputra: If empty, how can letting go be noble?

Subhuti: Noble is what has origins.

Manjushri: Not merely has; but abides in the origins of its nature.

Shariputra: Hence genuine letting go consists in this: in his very nature the bodhisattva belongs to the dharmadhatu. Thus he is released into it.

Subhuti: And not occasionally but prior to everything.

Shariputra: But I cannot really think of what is prior . . .

Manjushri: . . . because the nature of thinking begins there.

Shariputra: Thus the nature of the bodhisattva is released into the dharmadhatu in that which is before thought.

9

Subhuti: Clearly the nature of the bodhisattva is released into the dharmadhatu because his nature belongs so essentially to the dharmadhatu. Without the bodhisattvic nature the dharmadhatu could not be as it is.

Shariputra: This is hardly thinkable!

Manjushri: It cannot be thought of at all as long as we want to conceive of it as an objective, concrete relationship between an object called "bodhisattva" and an object called "dharmadhatu."

10

Subhuti: In the origins of his nature the bodhisattva abides absorbed in the letting go of the dharmadhatu. Abiding in his origins the bodhisattva is struck by what is noble in his nature. He surmises noble-mindedness.

Shariputra: And this surmising is waiting; for the absorption of letting go has been thought of as waiting.

Subhuti: If the dharmadhatu is the ground of all, then of all things patience can extend the furthest; it can surmise even the whole of the ground because it can wait the longest.

Manjushri: Patient noble-mindedness is the pure reposing in itself of that desire, which, abandoning desire, penetrates desirelessness.

I I

Manjushri: The meaning of this discourse is that the bodhisattva is coming near to and at the same time remaining
distant from the dharmadhatu.

Subhuti: And this is the meaning of both waiting and letting
go.

Shariputra: What is this nearness and distance within which
the dharmadhatu approaches and withdraws?

Subhuti: This nearness and distance can be nothing other
than the dharmadhatu.

Manjushri: Because the dharmadhatu is present in everything. It gathers everything together and lets everything
return to itself in its very own repose. It gathers, just as if
nothing were happening, each to each and each to all into
an abiding while reposing in itself. The dharmadhatu is the
ground of all which, gathering everything, opens itself so
that in it openness is held and secured, letting everything
unfold in its own repose.

Shariputra: Then the dharmadhatu itself is the nearing and
the distancing.

Subhuti: The dharmadhatu itself is the nearness of the distance and the distance of the nearness.

I 2

Ever to the bodhisattva child night neighbors the stars;
With neither seam nor edge nor thread she binds together.
She neighbors: she works with nearness alone;
Or in the depth of the heights, does she rest in wonder?
Can wonder open what is locked?

Only if it be released through waiting
And the bodhisattva remains
Rooted in that from whence he is called.

6

Unpredictable Moments

Imagine lying on a hilltop. You are gazing at the overcast sky, waiting for the clouds to thin out or break apart. They are gray but slowly and quietly moving. There is nothing you can do to make them separate. Any effort is futile. No matter what state of mind you are in, the clouds will open at their own time and the sun will shine through. Does personal effort play no role at all? The more prepared and waitful you are, the more you will be able to benefit from the breaking open of the clouds. So effort is the perseverance to wait. And perseverance in waiting is patience. If you are impatient, you will become distracted and disturbed, insensitive to what might happen at any moment. Then the moment will pass you by. The break in the clouds will go unnoticed. They will close again as silently and inconspicuously as they opened.

TECHNIQUE AND TECHNOLOGY

A technique is the embodiment of a logical procedure. In employing a technique, we apply a series of interconnected stages which have been thought out beforehand. Each stage is linked causally to the next. As long as we follow correctly the various stages, we will produce a predictable result. Thus a technique is a sequence of connected ideas, which when correctly applied produce an identical result under all circumstances.

Technology is essentially linked to technique. As such technology is not a recent or modern development. In the West, technology has been concerned with the application of techniques as a means to transform the material world. In the East, technology has been used as a method to transform the spiritual world. Whenever a technique is applied, a technology is presupposed. In this sense technology has nothing to do with scientific research and machinery: it refers to a particular approach to reality. Whether that reality be "outside" or "inside" oneself is irrelevant.

Any spiritual path that speaks of a series of interconnected stages leading to awakening, which can be followed under all or at least most human conditions, has a technological aspect. It will assume a causal and linear relationship between our present state (that of an unawakened being) and a higher, more evolved state (that of an awakened being). The latter is produced by transforming the former through applying a series of techniques (ethical disciplines, meditations, rituals etc.). The stuff of spiritual technology is spirit; whereas the stuff of material technology is matter. But both technologies assume that something can be transformed through the effective application of techniques.

Preoccupation with technique gives rise to a technical attitude. This is an orientation to life and the world. It assumes that reality is reducible to a certain number of elements which each have a particular place and function. Once the location, duration and type of the elements have been established, then it is possible to reorganize them into another order, or even to change them into something else. With faith in guidelines and instructions, we can then project an alternative (inner or outer) reality and proceed to realize it through applying the correct techniques. A technical attitude is thus a calculative one. It proceeds with conviction in the validity of its own knowledge and expectations.

> *Those that would gain what is under heaven by tampering*
>> *with it—I have seen that they do not succeed.*
> *For that which is under heaven is like a holy vessel,*
>> *dangerous to tamper with.*
> *Those that tamper with it, harm it.*
> *Those that grab at it, lose it.*[1] —Lao Tzu

I can see for myself that a technical approach to transforming the material world works. Yet even here what works on one level is often achieved only at a greater cost on another. Many advances in technology have brought unforeseen, destructive consequences in their wake. To submit nature to man's technical desires cannot be achieved without consequences that may cause more harm in the long term than any benefits produced in the short term. A technical attitude is locked in a narrow vision which is blind to the wider implications of its actions. It considers only the causal relations between things that may be exploited to fulfill its own desires. But it ignores their deeper interconnections:

*Broadly, we might say that man's increasing mastery
over nature has been accompanied . . . by a more and
more complete capitulation of man before his own fears
and desires, or even before the ungovernable element in
his nature. Man's mastery over nature, then, is a mastery
which has less and less control over itself . . . . A world
where techniques are paramount is a world given over to
desire and fear; because every technique is there to serve
some desire or fear.*[2] —Gabriel Marcel

Then could a spiritual technology also have unforeseeable
consequences that in the long term may cancel out its benefits? As a result of excessive application of spiritual techniques, could we end up with a kind of spiritual pollution?
In an exclusive devotion to technique, do we not overlook
something essential?

Gradual and Sudden Paths

For many centuries in China a controversy is said to have
raged between the adherents of the gradual and sudden paths
to awakening. The gradualists emphasized the need to train
systematically to produce a progressive transformation from
the state of an unawakened to an awakened being. For the
proponents of the sudden path awakening was present right
here and now; it was just a question of allowing it to erupt.

*There are moments of the secret ground in which world
order is beheld as present. Then the tone is heard all of a
sudden whose uninterpretable score the ordered world is.*

These moments are immortal; none are more evanescent.
They leave no content that could be preserved, but their
force enters into the creation and into man's knowledge,
and the radiation of its force penetrates the ordered world
and thaws it again and again.[3] —Martin Buber

The gradual path operates through the application of techniques, whereas the sudden path suggests something beyond the range of techniques. However, a gradual path nearly always includes unknown and indeterminate factors *(karma,* for example) which play an important role in the successful outcome of the practice. It is understood that even if one's practice is technically perfect, there is still no guarantee that the desired result of insight will be realized.

Even in a gradual conception of the path, the success of a spiritual technique requires the basis of a firm spiritual ground. This ground needs to be free from overtly unwholesome habits and endowed with ethical integrity. We are born with a given spiritual ground which plays an important part in our spiritual growth. Although we are free to purify and strengthen this ground, it remains essentially unknown and indeterminate. We can never really know our deepest strengths and weaknesses. We can never know what frightening abyss may lurk around the next corner, or what unimagined powers may await us.

So a gradual path does have an unpredictable element. But its unpredictability is due to the unknown and indeterminate spiritual ground upon which the path is based. In the sudden path the unpredictable has to do with the goal itself. What may suddenly and unexpectedly break through is not any unknown positive or negative potential, but awakening itself. The sudden path asserts that awakening can break into our lives at any moment.

> *If you want to understand the principle of the shortcut,*
> *you must blanket the one thought and suddenly break*
> *through it—then and only then will you comprehend*
> *birth and death. This is called the access to awakening.*
> *You should not retain any thought which waits for that*
> *breakthrough to occur, however. If you retain a thought*
> *which waits for a breakthrough, then you will never*
> *break through for an eternity of eons. You need only lay*
> *down, all at once, the mind full of deluded thoughts and*
> *inverted thinking, the mind of logical discrimination,*
> *the mind which loves life and hates death, the mind of*
> *knowledge and views, interpretation and comprehen-*
> *sion, and the mind which rejoices in stillness and turns*
> *from disturbance.*[4] —Ta Hui

The gradual path has the full support of reason on its side. But this makes it difficult for it to appreciate the irrational dimension of spiritual life. The sudden approach has little confidence in reason and finds itself mired in contradictions and imprecisions when forced to articulate itself. But it seems to be more open to the unpredictable and mysterious. The two sides speak two different languages. Their respective weaknesses are revealed because life contains both voices. No matter how loud one voice shouts, it will never drown out the other. They both have the same right and need to speak.

In practice, then, the path we follow will be both gradual and sudden. As the Zen tradition matured, its teachers realized that it was not a question of choosing one path as opposed to the other. Life is made up of both. As long as we live in time, subject to the laws of cause and effect, then our spiritual life will have a gradual dimension. Through living in a certain way, by doing certain practices, we will slowly change and evolve. Whatever we do will produce an effect. But every moment we are also prone to the breakthrough of sudden insight. Whatever we do, we can never be sure what will happen next.

BUDDHA AND BUDDHA-NATURE

From the gradualist's point of view, the suddenist's claim that Buddhahood is already present within us seems quite illogical. Surely Buddhahood entails insight into the nature of reality and boundless compassion for sentient beings. But how can such insight and compassion be said to be present if there is no consciousness of them? To speak of them as present, then surely they must be conscious. And how could an unawakened state and an awakened state coexist within a single person? If one is really a Buddha, then one cannot be an unenlightened sentient being—and vice versa. To claim that the unawakened is awakened contradicts that fundamental axiom of logic, the law of the excluded middle.

> *Therefore, we know that, unawakened, even a Buddha is a sentient being, and that even a sentient being, if awakened in an instant of thought is a Buddha . . . . The*

*Buddha mind is possessed by sentient beings, apart from
sentient beings there is no Buddha mind.*[5] —Hui Neng

It is far more reasonable to conceive of Buddha-nature in
terms of *potential*. To say that all sentient beings are endowed
with Buddha-nature simply means that they all have the
possibility of becoming Buddhas. At present they are not
Buddhas for the simple reason that they are unenlightened
and selfish, devoid of the qualities of Buddhahood. Buddha-
nature is just the potential for awakening. To realize this
potential, sentient beings need to embark on a systematic
course of training which will gradually transform them into
Buddhas.

*Suddenly the time arrives: you may be on a story of an
ancient's entry into the path, or it may be as you are reading the scriptures, or perhaps during your daily activities
as you respond to circumstances; whether your condition is good or bad, or your body and mind are scattered
and confused, whether favorable or adverse conditions
are present, or whether you have temporarily quietened
the mind's conceptual discrimination—when you suddenly topple the key link, there'll be no mistake about it.*[6]
—Ta Hui

There are numerous instances, and not merely in the
Buddhist tradition, where without any warning people have
been suddenly gripped by an unprecedented perception of
themselves and their world. Words hopelessly fail to recount
the depth and range of these experiences. But without hesi-

tation many would say that Buddhahood itself was present in that moment. The experience is such that any other name would be inadequate. The Zen tradition makes this claim explicit: you are already a Buddha—don't search for it anywhere else, just awaken to your own true nature! Buddhahood is not a remote and distant goal for which we have a mere potential. Right now Buddhahood is active and alive in the innermost heart of our lives.

> *Just because it's so very close, you cannot get this truth out of your own eyes. When you open your eyes it strikes you, and when you close your eyes it's not lacking either. When you open your mouth you speak of it, and when you shut your mouth it appears by itself. But if you try to receive it by stirring your mind, you've already missed it by eighteen thousand miles.*[7] —Ta Hui

Buddhahood is simultaneously far away and nearby. There is nothing further away from and nothing closer to us than Buddhahood. It is this paradox of nearness and distance that underscores the dilemma between the gradual and sudden approaches. The gradual orientation emphasizes the extreme distance of awakening, the sudden its extreme nearness.

From the standpoint of reason, Buddhahood represents the optimal mode of human evolution. It is the distant effect for which we are the cause. But in the light of the sudden experience this rational view is disregarded: Buddhahood is realized to be right here, closer to us than even our sense of "I."

Buddha, Buddhahood, and Buddha-nature are all inadequate names which can only point by analogy to what is inexpressible. Although unnameable, it calls out to be spoken. But words fail; they stick in your throat and remain glued to the tip of your tongue. "To say it is like something is not to the point."

> *"There is one thing which supports the heavens above and the earth below. It exists during all activity, but it is not confined to that activity. All of you! What do you call it?"* *Shen Hui came forward from the assembly and said, "It is the original source of all the Buddha's and Shen Hui's own Buddha-nature."* *[Hui Neng] said, "Even if I call it 'one thing' it is still not correct. How dare you call it 'original source' or 'Buddha-nature?' From now on, even if you go and build a thatched hut to cover your head, you will only be a follower of the school of conceptual understanding."*[8] —Hui Neng

Consider the Buddha-nature as a kind of awareness. To say that we all possess Buddha-nature could mean that we are all aware (perhaps very dimly) of a dimension of depth and mystery at the root of our lives. To be drawn to a meditative attitude implies an acknowledgment of this Buddha-awareness. Even without being able to formulate it, we suspect the presence of something far greater than our limited egos at the heart of our lives. The aim of the practice, then, is to bring this latent awareness to greater consciousness. This would imply that our present awareness of Buddha-nature (or Buddha-nature's awareness of itself) is largely unconscious. In psychological terms, it is disconnected from the ego-complex. It surfaces into the lake of consciousness sporadically and uncontrollably.

Buddha-nature as awareness or wisdom cannot be the object of any technical shaping or molding. We can have no technical grasp of Buddha-nature as such. Why? Because we can never extricate ourselves from it. We cannot turn Buddha-nature into a problem that confronts us as something to be unravelled or solved. Language plays tricks here. Buddha-nature can never stand before one as though it were a grammatical object connected by means of an act (verb) to oneself (subject). So to what extent is a technical attitude prefigured in the subject-verb-object structure of language? Are the very divisions presupposed in language not a precondition for the illusion of technique?

Language is inadequate when it attempts to talk of Buddha-nature. For non-poetic language, with its conceptual divisions, is restricted to the calculable world. To talk of Buddha-nature as wisdom or awareness is just another approximation, an expedient. Buddha-nature would not be what it is were it actually a state of awareness or wisdom. When we talk of such "things," we clothe them in what seems to resemble them most closely. Wisdom, as we know it, is not a quality of Buddha-nature, but just an appropriate symbol for it. It points to it as an analogy, while mysteriously partaking in what it is.

To say you are related to Buddha-nature is equally misleading. For every category of relation is drawn from what is already known and experienced. It is not the cause for which we are the effect; it is not the substance for which we are the accidents; nor is it a You for whom we are an I. Only symbolically can these relationships be used to describe our connectedness to Buddha-nature. So perhaps it is utterly transcendent—but even that would not be true. For transcendence only makes sense in comparison with immanence. And Buddha-nature is just as immanent as it is transcendent. Words fail. But as we wait in unknowing, as we poise ourselves to receive its unpredictable gestures, the silence becomes ever more articulate.

Unpredictable Moments

You cannot approach it with any certainty. All your longing and striving to realize something, to attain some insight are essentially futile. You cannot even speak of progress, for progress implies that you are getting closer to the goal. But you cannot get any closer than you already are. Certainty, longing, striving, progress—all of these are meaningful only in the realm of techniques. But it is outside the reach of any technique; it is "meta-technical." The moments in which it comes to you are unpredictable.

> *The world which appears to you in this way is unreliable, for it appears always new to you, and you cannot take it by its word. It lacks density, for everything in it permeates everything else. It lacks duration, for it comes even when not called and vanishes even when you cling to it. It cannot be surveyed: if you try to make it surveyable, you lose it. It comes—comes to fetch you—and if it does not reach you or encounter you it vanishes, but*

*it comes again, transformed. It does not stand outside
you, it touches your ground . . . . It does not help you to
survive; it only helps you to have intimations of eternity.*[9]
—Martin Buber

If I no longer see meditation as a simple application of
techniques, then I can no longer approach its practice with
the same kind of confidence with which I deal with technical matters. I have to accept that there is no certainty of
gaining a desired result merely by applying a set of instructions. To adopt such a meditative attitude is therefore a risk,
an unavoidable risk. I can appeal to no amount of past cases
in the history of the tradition to secure any assurance that its
techniques will also work in my case.

*The measure of the wisdom of universal brightness is
equal to the dharmadhatu or to all of space. It has neither
center nor edges. Its essence is the same as the mind of
all sentient beings. At what should you look? To what
dharma should you listen? In the worlds of the ten directions, that wisdom constantly appears to beings who have
affinities for it, and it never neglects the proper time.*[10]
—Li T'ung Hsüan

If technique is denied as the principal agent in giving rise
to spiritual experience, am I not obliged to acknowledge
the "instrumental" power of something meta-technical?
For surely the very notion of sudden awakening implies the
presence of something beyond the range of technique? But
how am I connected to this thing that is always present yet

without warning can break into the ordered everydayness of my life? It is as though it breathes within me with its own silent and barely perceptible breath, only suddenly to unleash gusts and gales of unsettling ferocity. It is futile to try and attain some preconceived fantasy of awakening. All I can do is create the conditions under which there is the greatest chance of it graciously deigning to happen.

> *I said to my soul, be still, and wait without hope*
> *For hope would be hope for the wrong thing; wait*
>   *without love*
> *For love would be love of the wrong thing; there is yet faith*
> *But the faith and the love and the hope are all in the*
>   *waiting.*
> *Wait without thought, for you are not yet ready for thought:*
> *So the darkness shall be the light, and the stillness the*
>   *dancing.*[11] —T.S. Eliot

What does it mean to say that I "cultivate" a spiritual quality such as patience, compassion, or wisdom? Can they be created just by applying techniques and through the force of will? Even if they are so produced, there must be something, some predisposition, that turns into patience, compassion, or wisdom. Or are they produced from nothing? Or from emptiness? Or are they already lying there dormant and complete, waiting to be exposed and freed? Again the mystery of Buddha-nature: is it sheer potentiality or latent wholeness? Or somehow a mixture of the two? A meditative attitude is maieutic, akin to a midwife. It neither designs nor constructs, but brings forth with care what is about to be born.

Essentially, you should always have faith that your own physical, verbal and mental states and all your different impulses arise from the Buddha's physical, verbal and mental states, and all his different impulses. They are all without essence or nature, without self or person. Since they all arise from the non-productive conditions of the own nature of the dharmadhatu, you cannot find a place where their roots were originally planted. Their nature itself is the dharmadhatu; there is no inside, outside, or in-between.[12] —Li T'ung Hsüan

I walked up to the ridge overlooking the monastery and finally calmed down. In a sense the meditation had started taking over, as if it had a power of its own. The world and everything I believed in seemed horribly tentative. I realized that were a "breakthrough" to occur, it would imply a completely new standpoint apart from anything I could conceive of. And that is frightening. Because—despite all the lofty talk about "transformation" and "awakening" do I seriously want to change? Do I not just want an appendage of enlightenment to stick on to what I already am? I understood that so many of my visions for the future were just extensions of my mediocre self covered with the veneer of misconstrued notions of sagacity. I even became afraid of the power of meditation and wished for my usual sleepy and distracted state of mind to return.

You must doubt deeply, again and again, asking yourself what the subject of hearing could be. Pay no attention to the various illusory thoughts and ideas that may occur

to you. Only doubt more and more deeply, gathering
together in yourself all the strength that is in you, with-
out aiming at anything or expecting anything in advance,
without intending to be enlightened and without even
intending not to intend to be enlightened; become like a
child in your own breast.[13] —Takasui

In acknowledging a meta-technical element as central to meditative practice, I am drawn closer and closer to a position akin to theism. God becomes ever more intelligible as soon as technique is rejected as an adequate spiritual path.

I have sometimes said that there is a power in the mind,
the only one that is free. Sometimes I have said that it is
a guardian of the mind; sometimes I have said that it is a
light of the mind; sometimes I have said that it is a spark.
Here is what I say now: it is neither this nor that, and yet
it is a something. It is raised above this and above that,
higher than the sky is above the earth . . . . It is free of all
names and devoid of all forms, entirely bare and free, as
void and free as God is in himself. It is perfect unity and
simplicity as God is unity and simplicity, so that in no
way can one peer into it.[14] —Meister Eckhart

If I deny the presence of something transcendent which can impinge upon and affect me unpredictably, I am bound to reduce spiritual practice to the application of techniques. A spiritual attitude, it seems, must acknowledge something that is both transcendent yet active in the world. In understanding Buddhism, it is crucial to establish the extent to which its practice depends and does not depend upon the application of techniques. How is the numinous, the uncanny, the mysterious approached? Awakening cannot be systematically cranked out as though it were the end-result of a technical procedure.

> *In the first place it would be absurd, not to say crazy, to suppose that there exists some technique, that is, some combination of methods which can be defined in abstract terms, by means of which we could reawaken love in souls that appear dead. Quite summarily, we have to say that such a reawakening can only be the work of grace, that is, something which is at the opposite pole to any sort of technique.*[15] —Gabriel Marcel

What is that seemingly final authority within me to which I appeal when judging the value or validity of spiritual claims? I judge people—by their presence and their words—to embody a degree of spiritual maturity. Somehow I find myself able to say that such and such a statement, utterance, poem etc. is more or less profound than another. But what is the measuring stick against which I pass these judgments? It is not anything rational or logical: this is less profound *because* . . . No. I judge something to be more or less significant because it resonates within me—at a level which I cannot clearly perceive myself—at a certain "pitch." This is putting it very crudely. But how else? Could there be a spiritual "scale" within me which corresponds to the entire spectrum of possible experience?

The less awake or conscious I am, the more this scale is

withdrawn and concealed. The path could then be thought of as bringing this scale to light. Perhaps this is the Buddha-nature again, from a different angle.

What I am writing here need not be a presumptuous claim to express something that I now "know." It may be that I will only understand later on what I write now. Perhaps I will never understand it. Creativity is an openness to something far greater than anything which can be reduced to the narrow confines of ego-consciousness. It is in no way a system of duplication, of expressing externally what is already formed in the silent, invisible interiors of my soul. That which is created is never entirely known beforehand. I can only intuit its preliminary stirrings. The words or images that come forth are molded in the act of creation itself. The work is a mystery from beginning to end.

The origination of all things is entirely creative. There is nothing which passes from a hidden state of latency into actuality. Whatever exists originates neither from itself nor from anything other than itself. It is entirely new, but without in any way being disconnected.

Although I am intimately woven into the fabric of life, I am simultaneously free to move about within it. This is a seeming contradiction; but an inevitable one. My inseparability from the world need not imply the fixed idea of everything being just mind; and my separation from the world does not imply that countless self-existent things stand rigidly against me.

The sun, the earth, the moon, and the stars: it was as if the entire universe were collaborating in my insignificant existence. Now only the clasp of egoism prevents this awareness. The turning inwards of meditation allows me to become aware of the universe itself flowing within and through me. Like a fish being swept along with the current of a river I am unaware of what gives me life. But by turning back against the current, for the first time I can feel it. In this sense meditation goes against the usual flow of things. But once this flow has been touched, I need always to resist whatever forces attempt to isolate me from it again.

> *But if you suddenly recognize that there is no self and penetrate deeply into the emptiness of material things, subject and object will both be obliterated. What then will remain to be realized? It is as if a particle of dust were thrown into a fiercely howling wind or a light boat were to flow with a swift current.*[16]
> —Yung Ming Yen Shou

I lie in wait for those moments when the mysterious starts to permeate everything, weaving its subtle course through all things and imbuing them with its shimmer. No methods can produce an awareness of this. The most I can do is be prepared and receptive for such an awareness to manifest.

> *There is a part of our being to which strange, perhaps not altogether conceivable, conditions give us sudden access; the key is in our hands for a second; and a few minutes later the door is shut again and the key disappears.*[17]
> —Gabriel Marcel

Make your will one! Don't listen with your ears, listen with your mind. No, don't listen with your mind, but listen with your spirit. Listening stops with the ears, the mind stops with recognition, but spirit is empty and waits on all things. The Tao gathers in emptiness alone. Emptiness is the fasting of the mind.[18] —Chuang Tzu

Since one who enters the dharmadhatu enters nowhere, there is nowhere he does not enter. Since one who cultivates the boundless qualities gained through practice actually gains nothing, there is nothing he does not gain.[19]
—Ch'eng Kuan

As I sit upright on the seat of the middle way at the reality limit,
What has been unmoving since of old is called Buddha.[20]
—Uisang

When the Light in Your Eyes Falls
to the Ground

We had been meditating for about a month when it happened. I had been at Songgwang Sa for nearly three years; this was my sixth retreat. It was a cold, dry winter. The ground of the courtyard was starting to freeze, crack, and, in places, sink. Biting winds were blowing dust throughout the monastery, coating with a brown veil the ice that gripped the nearby river. At six that evening we had performed our short service of three bows in the meditation hall and were preparing to sit until nine. But at twenty past six they rang the main bell (I remember glancing at my watch). It rang seventy-four more times. Each deep note took many long seconds to unravel its lingering tones.

With each successive note I realized with mounting certainty that Kusan Sunim had died. One by one we stood up from our cushions and paced around the hall. It was as if the pressure of the bell were too unsettling to be contained in stillness: the echoes of each stroke spread into my belly and limbs and forced me to move. The monastery was roused. I could hear hesitant voices enquiring, seeking yet not wanting confirmation. I heard feet walking and running, doors and gates opening and closing, the silence of the evening broken.

I had last seen him six days before when we went to visit him with Jagwang. We had entered his dimly lit room. He lay stretched out on the warm floor, cushioned by a thin mattress. He was barely recognizable. His head was supported by a hard, cylindrical pillow. His skin was taut and yellow, with no hint of the youthful luster that had shone from him in spite of his years. The flesh on his arms had withered, become senile and trembling. His shaven head was just a membrane-covered skull. His cheeks were sunken and the eyes gazed hugely from their hollows. His right arm lay over the blanket. Between his thumb and forefinger he slowly turned a small rosary with beads the size of walnuts. The beads fell in soft clicks.

The strokes had left him paralyzed on the left side of his body. He could barely move, talk, or swallow. Yongjin was his attendant then. He nursed him day and night: feeding, cleaning, and massaging him. But there was no melancholy or despair in the room. The old man was becoming a child again, a child in whom the weight of experience was settled like a rock.

Yongjin sat him up and knelt behind him, cradling him in his arms. He caressed his scalp and held his head to prevent it from lurching about. We bowed three times and knelt before him, confused with embarrassment and respect. Was he even aware of us? He murmured something, opened his eyes, and stared at us with a childlike gaze. Songil went over and sat beside him, and he turned his head towards her. For several minutes (or was it seconds?) she exchanged something wordless with him through her eyes.

The bell was still ringing when the nine of us assembled
in the courtyard in front of the hall. We had put on our formal gowns and robes and stood in a group waiting to go up
to his room. We shuffled around, both to keep warm and
to avoid each other. Across the courtyard wall I could hear
other monks, alone and in groups, hurrying up the path to
his quarters.

We walked in single file through the tile-covered gate
and up the path to his room. A single lamp flickered across
the sad and bewildered faces of the monks gathered in front
of the building. When I entered the room, I was shocked
by its transformation. Electric lights glared onto the bare,
ochre-colored floor. Solemn figures in gray and brown robes
stood in harsh relief against the white walls. At the end of
the room a black folding screen, the one with a sutra written
in tiny golden characters, zig-zagged across the floor. We
lined up and bowed in unison. Then Yongjin impatiently
beckoned us to come and see the body behind the screen.

My mind was so numbed by all this that I can hardly
remember now what I saw. I peered behind the screen. Fully
robed, his slumped body was seated clumsily on a chair. A
narrow strip of white cloth circled his head and was knotted
at the crown. His face . . . I suppose I was disappointed by
his face. It was as though the light had gone out of his eyes.

That evening at nine we began the vigil that was to last
until the funeral in four days' time. I was relieved it would
not entail the ringing of bells and the droning of sutras. It
was to be a stark, dignified affair. The monks were divided
into groups of five and a rota worked out so that each group
would supervise the vigil for four hours a day at five hourly
intervals. Each group was to sit in silent meditation before

the screen. We were to enter, bow, and wait for the preceding group to leave, and take its place on the five square cushions lined across the center of the room. Three sharp strokes of the clapper would signal the beginning and end of the session.

The normal schedule of the three month winter retreat was suspended. Day and night were concentrated around these four hours of meditation before the screen, an improvised altar and a steadily accumulating mass of flowers. As I sat I listened to the sounds made by people as they entered the room, lit a stick of incense, bowed, and tiptoed out. His Korean disciples, who had appeared from all over the country, sat along one side of the room. For hours on end they meditated, dozed, and gazed dumbly at the floor. Each time a visitor came in, they stood up to receive bows: wordless consolation for their grief.

As the vigil drew to a close, those coming to pay their respects had increased to such proportions that the body, now encased in an L-shaped coffin to fit its newly acquired lotus posture, was humped out of his room down to a larger hall in the monastery. It was hidden behind another altar covered with fruits, nuts, sweets, beans, pounded-rice cakes, flowers, and wreaths. These riches clustered around a large, ornately framed photograph from which he permanently smiled. Buses arrived from Seoul, Pusan, and other towns to disgorge huddles of monks and nuns, lines of middle-aged and ancient women dressed in gray, and solitary businessmen and bureaucrats whose Western suits complained with ugly creases as they lowered themselves to the floor.

His Korean disciples insisted that we foreigners stay with

them to meditate throughout the final night of the vigil. To begin with the hours passed easily and a deep tranquility settled over the room. Images of the old man drifted into my mind, froze, and then vanished. I saw him sitting in his room wrapped in a hooded, black cloak; looking curiously at a Burmese scripture written on thin slats of wood; sitting stern and inscrutable, his eyes aglow, with a staff by his side during interviews; bounding down the steep, stone staircase behind the Buddha-hall; squatting in the forest pruning pine saplings we were about to plant. But when midnight passed, this stillness and clarity slipped into torpor. My perception faded and my senses watched helplessly as streams of images bombarded my numb mind.

I wandered out of the muggy room into the courtyard. The shock of the icy, moonlit night revived me. I looked around and saw rows of neatly stacked collapsible chairs and what looked like a white proscenium arch erected in front of the monastery's museum. A couple of figures were strolling about. An old lady sat half-asleep in one of the chairs like the forgotten member of an audience still contemplating a vacant stage.

When the watery sun rose over the mountains some hours later, the courtyard was already buzzing with preparations for the ceremony. The arch now contained a three-tiered altar draped with white cotton and adorned with the customary offerings of food, flowers and incense. "KU SAN TAE SON SA" was painted in bold Chinese characters across the front of the arch. Huge circular wreaths of concentric rings of yellow and white chrysanthemums, offered by heavy industries and generals, stood on trestles to either side. (Even the Presbyterian dictator had one sent in his name.) The chairs had been unfolded and placed in horizontal rows facing the altar. The loudspeaker system spluttered and shrieked as it was tested. Monks dashed about, their breath condensing in the freezing air, their robes hastily gathered, clutching pieces of paper, and shouting instructions.

The abbot strode into the hall where the body sat waiting and called for attention. Immediately, a cluster of disciples braced themselves and shot behind the screen. The monk we called "Cowboy" extracted a hammer from somewhere in his robes and secured with nails a cord of plaited cloth around the coffin. Then they gripped the cord and raised the box from the floor, exposing beneath it several lazily fuming chunks of dry ice. They shuffled towards the door, their bodies contorted as they struggled to manage their clumsy load.

They stumbled out of the hall into the blinding winter sunlight. A small procession formed in front of and behind them. They carried the body through the monastery grounds, accompanied by the knocking of a wooden-fish and the languid chanting of Amitabha's name. With every step, more figures in gray were drawn to the procession as though by the magnetic tug of the coffin. At last they pulled up behind the altar in the courtyard. They laid the coffin on a wooden bier and placed over it a large, rectangular, polystyrene casing that had been meticulously studded with chrysanthemums.

I had never seen such a huge throng of people in the monastery before. A sea of faces flooded the courtyard and spilled onto every available vantage point. In the front rows

sat monastic dignitaries, government officials, military offi-
cers, and wealthy benefactors (including one old lady who
guiltily removed her mink stole when she came forward to
offer incense). We foreigners were placed among the tightly
packed rows of monks that formed two arcs connecting the
front row of chairs with the ends of the altar, sealing off the
space where the ceremonies were to be conducted.

A pack of expressionless photographers and video-
technicians swooped in unison upon every visual moment:
the weeping disciples; the chanting monks; men and women
placing flowers and incense on the altar; people reading
speeches, recollections and tributes; and the group of girls
who sang mournful, piercing songs. For more than an hour
the crowd stood in silence, motionless except for a slight
swaying to free their feet from the frozen ground. The sun
blazed but with little warmth. I felt a strange collective sorrow being simultaneously fueled and assuaged by the words
and gestures of the ceremony.

When the last grains of incense had been sprinkled into
the censer, the crowd surged around the altar as a score of
strong young monks eased the bier onto their shoulders and
began a final circumambulation of the courtyard. Again
the main bell was struck. Banners of colored satin, strung
from bamboo poles, glittered wildly in the sunlight and converged to form the head of a procession. The bier returned,
now trailing two long plaits of coarsely woven white cloth
that were carried over the shoulders of those who followed
it. The stillness of the crowd was abandoned to chatter and
shouts but this was gradually converted into fervent chanting by the insistent dok! dok! dok! of a wooden-fish.

The excited cortège struggled free of the courtyard and made its way down to the river. It cautiously wove across the narrow path of stepping-stones above the waterfall, then turned right down the path towards the village, past the twisting pines and the alarming gaze of the lichen-mottled dragons curled atop the rows of steles.

Further down the hill, it recrossed the river and, in the shade of a grove of tall, thin cypresses, climbed the rocky path behind the monastery farm. It came to the low ridge which looked out onto a glade of terraced rice fields carved into the wooded hillside. The bier was edged down to the bank of a stream, where it paused for a moment before winding across the shallow water to the higher levels of the stubble-covered terrace.

A fire pit had already been dug into the hard soil of the paddy. It was ventilated from below by an underground tunnel that had been bored into the retaining-wall of the terrace and surfaced through a terra-cotta chimney on the far side of the pit. It was packed with charcoal whose soft, black dust lingered over the ground. Kindling—bundles of forest bamboo, shreds of tree bark, and branches of freshly cut pine—lay heaped to one side. Chopped logs were stacked in careless piles, their splintered white innards exposed. And, half-concealed behind them, sat grubby canisters of kerosene.

The procession poured into the rice field, its banners gleaming against the blue sky. Monks swarmed around the pit to be quickly hemmed in by the pressing crowd of laity. A few yards away the bier was lowered to the ground. The casing of chrysanthemums was discarded and there sat the dull L-shaped coffin. A cluster of disciples gathered around it, raised it up and hauled it over to the pit. The crowd reluctantly parted as the coffin approached and then tightly closed again, as if to protect it. The charcoals crunched and squeaked as it landed.

The taut attention of hundreds of eyes focused on the L-shaped box. Under Cowboy's command, the disciples snatched kindling and logs and frantically buried the coffin beneath a heap of fuel. Then they sloshed kerosene over it all, piercing the air with its oily reek. The crowd was urged to stand back while two monks got ready to ignite the pyre with long sticks tipped with swabs of kerosene-soaked cloth that burned smokily and dripped tiny beads of fire. "Get out! Get out! It's burning! It's burning!" they shouted to the figure in the coffin. Then they stabbed at the pyre and straightaway flames licked at the smaller branches and twigs; bamboo leaves crackled; pine needles flared and hissed; and a pall of cumbersome gray smoke rose from the heart of the pyre and unfurled into the dazzling sky.

As the fire stampeded ahead, it dispersed the spectators with waves of smoke and replaced their murmurs and sobs with its own triumphant roar. Suddenly, a number of overwrought women in gray converged like a madly gathering flock of birds. One of them screamed that she had seen the old man's face gazing at her from the column of smoke. Then she broke down and wept. But it was over now. The crowd was drifting away, returning to a million other concerns. The banners lay abandoned around the edges of the field. Only a handful of people remained.

The conflagration became quieter yet fiercer, implacable

and content. The thick smoke that had welled from its foliage dissolved. The fire no longer had to impress us; it just burned with a steady, earnest heat. The scene at that moment is clearly etched in my mind. Facing me on the far side of the fire is a tall Korean monk, standing erect and passive. He quivers in the heat waves as though reflected in the flawed surface of a mirror. To my left the abbot kneels on the lip of the terrace, his hands clasped in supplication. On my right stands Robert, like a guard of honor at a medieval court, holding a bamboo pole from which a red banner sways in consort with the wisps of smoke.

A group of monks and villagers dragged several coarse, brown rush mats over to the pyre. They dampened them with water and then threw them over the fire, adjusting their positions with long wooden sticks so they completely covered the mass of burning wood and charcoal. A steaming hump of matting was soon all that stood out of the desolate field. Unable to escape, the fire searched deeper into its core, and reached for the body at its heart.

It was midafternoon. By unspoken, common consent, we walked slowly back to the monastery. No trace remained of the magnificent procession that had crowded along the same narrow path a few hours before. Only the tread of our feet, the faint rustle of bamboo, and the distant gurgle of the stream accompanied us. The courtyard was deserted now, the altar with its imposing arch was already half-dismantled and strewn across the ground. Battered wreaths lay in heaps among sheets of splintered plywood, paper bags and strips of cloth. The collapsible chairs clattered as they were loaded into the backs of trucks.

At dusk the glare of daylight subsided. A chill evening breeze rippled up the valley. The sky turned almost white, melting into a strip of watery orange above the hills in the west. Dressed in padded coats and woolen caps, we returned to the terraced field where the pyre continued to burn. Twenty or so people were gathered there, sitting, squatting, and standing around the fire.

The iridescent mass of combustion seemed to sink forever into the viscera of the earth. Its surface was partly covered by fragments of scorched matting. But where this shield-like crust was absent, tiny blue and yellow flames danced transparently upon a globe of orange heat. The fire was like the body of a coiled dragon. The chimney formed the dragon's neck and head. A stream of softly roaring flame issued from its mouth.

I am mesmerized by the fire. Its warmth glows upon our faces and instills a quiet conviviality among us. Its contours are transformed into a fiery landscape. I see mountains, valleys, and plains. The ground is burning orange, the ridges and hills charred and ragged. Yes, it resembles Mount Chogye. I can make out the peak, the steep slope that spreads out into the broad valley below and rises to the long ridge opposite that sweeps around the edge of the plateau, glittering with silvery plumes of pampas-grass.

I start to cry. The poor old man. The sickly sweetness of his flesh has been exhaled now. Only the elemental fragments of his life remain; but even they are being breathed away in the molten coals. His bones explode in clusters of crimson sparks. Deep in the soul of the furnace, I can discern pieces of the cranium and vertebrae. They are suspended, turning in slow motion, like alchemical ingredients in a cru-cible. Crouched together on the rim of the fire, our backs chilled by the night, we see the abbot walk toward us to wit-ness these final teachings.

As the orb of the moon reaches the apex of its course, the fire gathers more tightly into itself. Its glow is diminished by that of the rising moon which now shines on the surround-ing mountains, the forest, the irregular curves of the rice fields, and the figures huddled around their only source of warmth. Our glowing hands and faces turn from brilliant orange to dull red while our silhouettes become silver shapes on which shadows play.

Around half-past-three this tableau is shaken by the drone of the main bell as it announces the beginning of day in the monastery below. We stretch and yawn. A young monk stands up and starts to intone the morning service. The repetitive chanting enlivens us. When the service is over, a renewed silence settles over the landscape. But the cold becomes more bitter and we shiver, shuffling closer to the fire for warmth. And only then do we notice the immo-bile form of that old, thin monk, whom none of us had seen before, gazing impassively into the stirrings of the dying fire.

As daylight reluctantly filled the pale sky, we climbed back up the winding path to the terraced fields. The air was thick with a chill dampness. The huge white circle of the moon hung precariously over the end of the valley. The fire was no longer visible. I had to lean over it to feel its unsuspected heat rise from the pale brown and white ashes at the bot-tom of the pit. It had shrunk into the ground and now hid beneath its own detritus. The light of day diminished it; it cowered like some trapped nocturnal animal. A group of monks peered cautiously over the rim of the pit at the intricate confusion of its remains.

The ashen surface of the fire looked like that of a distant glacier. A profusion of finely wrought ridges in pristine shades of brown, white, and gray conflicted with the sooted chunks of soil and rock that clung to the slopes of the pit. I was puzzled by this confusion of detail and struggled to organize it into more familiar shapes and meanings. Suddenly, it made sense. Lying across the ridges, in a surreal distortion of scale, I saw ribs, vertebrae, and shards of human bone. They too possessed this strange, ashen purity, but also a terrible stubbornness in their refusal to be destroyed.

In the early afternoon, disciples wearing clean, white gloves reached into the pit and extracted the remains. They picked out the hot pieces of bone with chopsticks improvised from pieces of kindling that still lay scattered on the field, and dropped them onto a flat rock which they had dragged over to the side of the fire. Then they scooped up the ashes with a shovel and left them on trays to cool. As they dug further, they exposed a perforated, wrought iron grill, severely buckled by the heat. And below this twisted floor we glimpsed a smoldering carpet of bone and charcoal chips that had slipped through the holes of the grill.

When the extracted remains had cooled, the monks began to sift them with meticulous attention. A tightly packed, expectant crowd of onlookers teetered along the lip of the terrace above, straining their necks forward to see the pieces of bone as they were prodded and scratched, held to the light, and passed from one gloved hand to another. Some of the monks smiled to themselves and each other. The onlookers became restless and shouted questions to the monks who either didn't hear them or ignored them. Finally, Yongjin stood up and walked over to them. Four warped bone fragments were cupped protectively in his hands. Each piece was fired with strange, azure streaks. A gleeful murmur of approval rose from the onlookers. With gleaming eyes, they reverently studied the relics paraded before them.

That evening we were able to examine the remains more closely. By then most of the bone, charcoal, and ash had been taken back to his room and lay in heaps on newspapers and low, wooden tables. His skeleton had been shattered into hundreds of fragments by the heat. Each piece seemed so light and brittle. Only when I picked one up and pressed it between my fingers did I realize how hard and unbreakable it was, how sharp and jagged its edges. The disciples huddled in small groups around the room and picked through their little heaps of ash and bone. Some rested against the walls with outstretched legs as they worked, some peeled tangerines and inadvertently sprayed the remains with fine jets of juice, and others became engrossed by a story in one of the newspapers. If a piece of bone looked suspicious, it would be passed to the abbot who sat at a table in a bright pool of lamplight. There were three shallow saucers on his table. In each saucer were a number of tiny mineral-like droplets of different shapes and colors. The abbot would pick these up with a pair of tweezers and examine them against the light. Some were almost perfect spheres, some were oval. They were black and brown, pearl-white and transparent, sultry turquoise and even glistening sapphire-blue. It was as though the light from the old man's eyes had fallen to the ground and been magically transformed into the luster of these enigmatic little stones.

Songil and I left the room and walked into the darkness. It had started to rain. Drops of water fell heavily upon our umbrellas as we hurried along the forest path, drawn irresistibly back to where the fire still lingered. Farmworkers had erected a makeshift shelter above the pit to protect whatever relics still remained among the glowing coals. They had secured a blue tarpaulin over a bamboo frame and inside had somehow connected an electric light bulb from the farm below. It glared over the dry, bare soil that descended sharply into the pit. Two young monks sat quietly at the back on bundles of straw. The wind blew in fierce gusts from the hills and hurled rain against the flapping tarpaulin. The roof leaked and intermittent trickles of water dripped into the artificial cavern.

We crouched in the dust on the edge of the pit and stared at the gray carpet of ash and embers. We watched the last glowing fragments of charcoal flicker and die one by one. The heat of the fire had penetrated and clung to the earth. Now it slowly rose as a gentle tide of warmth into our chilled bodies. Time evaporated. We waited and listened as the night slipped away. It was like guarding an archaeological site where an ancient temple or shrine had been unearthed. This is what birth had once produced and death had now undone. It still showed itself and at the same time withdrew. The enigma reigned in everything, perplexing us. Even if he were only barely alive, it would be incalculably better than this. But having touched this abyss, it was unbearable to contemplate its ending, and the inevitable decline into the shallows of everyday life.

The next morning we crushed his bones. In front of the black and golden screen in his room an altar had been prepared on which the relics were now neatly displayed on discs of red velvet in sealed glass dishes. We bowed and sat still for a few minutes. Then we turned to where the heap of broken bones lay piled on a sheet of rice paper. To its side were two black roof tiles: one concave, wide and shallow, the other narrower and U-shaped. The abbot placed a handful of bones in the shallow tile, pressed the other on top and rolled it firmly from side to side, cracking and pulverizing the bones. We all took it in turns to kneel on the floor, grip the coarse edges of the tile and laboriously crunch these resistant fragments to dust.

We left the monastery in the early afternoon and followed the river upstream through the leafless forest to the high, distant ridges. The powdered bone had been wrapped in rice paper and placed inside a celadon vase. I kept my eyes on the bulbous shape of this urn as it distended the cotton knapsack of the young monk ahead who nimbly climbed the twisting path. We branched off into a smaller valley, leaving the familiar rush and gurgle of the river behind. The forest here was dense and silent. The long fingers of the straining trees reached like splinters into the anemic sky. The bamboo brush rattled as we waded through it chest-deep. Anonymous birds shrieked as we approached. The path became narrower and steeper. The straggling procession paused as

the elder monks sat on rocks, clasping their knees, gulp-
ing the cold, dry air. The trickle of even occasional rivulets
ceased. We clambered up the nearly precipitous face of the
ridge and finally stood above the forest, surveying the broad
valley that separated us from the squat peak of Mount Chogye rising on the far side of the massif.

The wind moaned and whistled across the broken pampas-
grass and through the knotted branches of the stunted trees,
stinging our frozen cheeks. We followed a winding path
between gaunt shrubs with brittle, russet leaves. This led us
to a clearing further up the valley at the foot of the hill that
rose to the peak. Roughly hewn stones lay scattered across
the ground, enmeshed in brambles. Some were blackened
with soot; others broken remnants of a water trough. This
was where his hermitage had been before the army ordered
its destruction as part of an anti-guerrilla campaign. The celadon vase was unpacked and placed on the ground among
the rubble and the weeds. Yongjin lit a stick of incense. We
stood in a line facing the absent hermitage and intoned a
brief prayer that was immediately obliterated by the wind.

Songil was squatting on the hillside cradling the vase
in her arms as we each came up and scooped some of the
coarse, white powder into a paper cone. We separated and
edged our ways up the pathless slope of the hill. I came to a
small clearing. Twisted thorns with large red berries clung
to the flinty soil. The sea in myriad inlets gleamed beyond
the fading purple and violet mountains. The peak of Mount
Chogye loomed above. The sky was huge and limpid. The
crushed bones dispersed in a tiny cloud as they were freed

from my outstretched fingers. A puff of white dust lingered for a moment before it was snatched away forever by the wind. The heavier particles crashed like a shower of rain onto the dead leaves.

Appendix
The Chinese Lesson

Now that Buddhism is establishing itself in countries previously dominated by Christian and European cultures, I am tempted to look back into the past and examine what happened when it entered other countries for the first time. Perhaps we can learn something by observing whether the difficulties we now face in understanding this foreign religion were encountered before. If so, how were these difficulties overcome? Were any mistakes made that we could avoid repeating? Yet the most we can glean from such comparison will be clues, pointers, and guidelines; for history is unlikely to repeat itself. And we should be aware that such comparative analysis may itself become a factor in determining the outcome of Buddhism's entry into the West.

Because of the vast cultural gulf between East and West, it may be argued that any comparative study of the movement of Buddhism from one Asian country to another will hardly be relevant to this present situation. But it is time that the principal assumption underlying this and similar arguments be laid to rest. The idea of the "East" as a cultural monolith is an illusion, a gross oversimplification reflecting both the indifference and vestigial imperial arrogance of the West towards Asia. India and China have both produced rich and complex cultures which are as different from each other as either of them are from the culture of Europe. In some respects, racially and linguistically, for example, India is even closer to Europe than it is to China. Instead of thinking in terms of "East" and "West," we should at least think in terms of three cultures: those of Europe, India, and China.

The Advent of Buddhism

During the early years of the Christian era, Buddhism moved from India along the trading routes of Central Asia to China. During the centuries that followed it established itself there and came to exert a powerful and enduring influence on numerous aspects of Chinese life. This is an historical example of Buddhism successfully moving between two countries separated by cultural differences as great as those between Europe and any country in Asia. When introduced into China, Buddhism encountered a sophisticated civilization with a long and independent history, as distinct from the less developed cultures it met in most other Asian countries. For these reasons, the assimilation and development of Buddhism in China provides the most relevant historical parallel to the current phenomenon of Buddhism's entry into the West.

Buddhism found fertile soil in the China of the second and third centuries because it spoke to the needs of a society in the midst of spiritual crisis. In 206 BCE the Han dynasty was established on the basis of the teachings of Confucius.

The founders of the dynasty believed that since these teachings were true, then a harmonious and just society should result from their application. In practice, though, things did not work out as planned and internal social and political conflicts eventually led to the break up of the dynasty in 220 CE and the catastrophic division of China in 317. Members of the former ruling and literate classes were forced into exile south of the Yangtse, an area considered a cultural backwater of the empire, and foreign invaders from Mongolia and elsewhere took control of the more civilized north. In addition to the loss of power and privilege, a keen sense of a loss of value and meaning was also experienced. The current turn of events unequivocally exposed the failure of a system of thought and practice that had sustained the Chinese spirit for the previous four hundred years.

Nearly two thousand years later Buddhism again finds itself in an alien culture confronted with a spiritual crisis. The loss of value and meaning experienced in the West has arisen from a number of causes, a principal one being the breakdown of the ancestral religion of Christianity. People find themselves in a spiritual vacuum, the traditional symbols and doctrines of their religion dismissed by a scientific and technological world view incapable of providing a satisfactory matrix of meaning. As in fourth century China, we experience a divided world, externally split by conflicting ideologies and internally torn apart by doubt and uncertainty. The fragmentation, despair, alienation, and nihilism of our times mirror the confusion of fourth century China and provide equally fertile soil for the advent of a foreign religion such as Buddhism.

The teachings of Buddhism attracted the disaffected intelligentsia of post-Han China in several ways. Instead of emphasizing the correct ordering of society on earth, as Confucianism had done, Buddhism stressed the importance of the individual's quest for liberation from a beginningless cycle of birth and death determined by one's own intentional actions *(karma)*. The moral value of a deed was decided not by the effect it had on contributing to or undermining the harmony of social relations, but by the consequences it would bear in a future life. Buddhism introduced the Chinese to the notion of the endurance of an individual destiny within a universe of almost infinite possibilities, in contrast to a short-lived career within unreliable social and political structures.

Ironically, perhaps, the religion renowned for its doctrine of no-self *(anatman)* provided the Chinese for the first time with a coherent philosophy of an individual self that was able to rise out of the ashes of the socio-centered teachings of Confucianism. The Chinese, like many in the West today, found it very difficult to reconcile the notion of no-self with those of *karma* and rebirth. If there is no self, then who or what passes from one birth to the next? How can "I" commit actions that "I" will experience in a future existence? And who or what enjoys the release of *nirvana?* Unlike the Indian Buddhists, for whom the idea of no-self stood against the backdrop of the deeply entrenched doctrines of self and *karma,* the Chinese were presented with the same ideas but in a context where a philosophy of self was almost totally lacking and the notion of karma and rebirth unheard of. What the Chinese sought was not a further negation to add to their already profound sense of privation, but the affirmation of something real and enduring. This could explain the great popularity in southern China of the *Mahaparinirvana Sutra,* translated into Chinese by Dharmakshema in 421, which instead of emphasizing no-self, taught the "eternal, joyous, personal and pure nature of nirvana." "That which is without self is life and death," it states, "but it is the self that is the Tathagata." Tao Sheng and Pao Liang, both renowned monks of the time, identified this "true self" with the Buddha-nature inherent in all sentient beings and regarded it as that which experiences the ineffable transcendence of *nirvana.*[1]

The Buddhist attitude to the self is equally baffling for us in the West today. On the one hand are those who see the doctrine of *anatman* not only as a potent remedy against the over-inflated ego that dominates the arrogant, aggressive, and selfish Western psyche, but also as a simple negation of self that posits nothing further. On the other hand are those who, often appealing to Mahayana and Chinese sources, talk of a Self with a capital "S" that is revealed once the obscurations of the ego are removed—or they simply elevate the Buddha-nature to the status of a substitute *atman.* One peculiar feature of our spiritual crisis is that we are simultaneously in search of a self and desirous of its elimination. We are looking for a soul in the midst of a soulless universe while dissatisfied with the contemporary substitutes of an alienated Cartesian *cogito* or a frustrated Freudian *ego.*

Ultimately, the way Buddhism offers out of the apparent self/no-self dilemma is not a philosophical but a practical, therapeutic one. The sanest and most enduring insights into the nature of who we are were reached by the Chinese through meditation (ch'an/zen) rather than theory. Lin Chi's remarkable "true person of no status," for example, is the uncontrived expression of an abrupt yet deeply revealing experience induced by forceful, even shocking methods. Yet it took Buddhism more than five hundred years of absorption into Chinese culture before it was sufficiently integrated to produce a truly Chinese form of Buddhism. This should serve as a sobering and humbling reminder to those of us who are already seeking to define the nature of Western Buddhism. Although our highly differentiated intellects and advanced communications technology may enable us to get a grasp of Buddhist theory much faster than the Chinese, the time it takes for a spiritual tradition to take root and flower in a foreign culture can never be greatly speeded up. Just because we better understand the principles of botany doesn't mean that we can make trees grow significantly faster than our ancestors.

As in the West today, Buddhism started in China among small, relatively isolated groups and had only a marginal effect on the life of society as a whole. Taoists were drawn to Buddhism because of the apparent similarities it bore with their own doctrines and practices. Lay intellectuals were attracted by its original and challenging philosophy and founded small circles who would meet, often with a learned monk, to discuss the implications of these new ideas. Monastic centers were established, initially to provide for the needs of Central Asian and Indian traders resident in China, and later to serve indigenous communities of Chinese Buddhists. A small but steady number of Indian and Chinese monks travelled between India and China, the former to teach and help translate texts, the latter to study Buddhism in its country of origin and return to impart their knowledge to their fellow countrymen. The parallels with our present situation are so obvious as to require no further comment. It will be interesting to see whether within a comparable period of time the speed of development will be similar: by the year 300 (about two hundred years after the first Chinese contacts with Buddhism) in the cities of Loyang and Ch'ang an alone there were 180 Buddhist establishments occupied by 3,700 monks and nuns.[2]

Buddhism expanded rapidly in China as soon as it was adopted by the ruling classes. In the northern states it was used by the foreign rulers because it was non-Chinese in origin, hence weakening the attachment of the subjugated peoples to their national ways of thinking, and because of its universalism that was able to supplant the tribal beliefs that were inadequate to the task of forging an empire.[3] In the south it found sympathy among the educated classes and wove its way into the literate and philosophical culture of the exiled Han court. Rulers and emperors were sometimes identified as *chakravartin,* or "(Dharma) wheel-turning" kings, or even as living Buddhas, thus greatly elevating the status of the religion and resolving any conflict in loyalty between sangha and state. As in every case in the past, the main reason Buddhism was able to make the transition from a fringe phenomenon to a significant force in society was because of its adoption by the ruling class and subsequent imposition upon the populace. Such imposition of a religion is not only highly unlikely but actually undesirable in the kind of secular democracy we live in today. If Buddhism is to have more than a marginal influence in contemporary Western societies, it will have to enter the cultural mainstream in unprecedented and unpredictable ways.

The first teachings to be imported into China were those concerning the basic Buddhist doctrines of suffering, rebirth, nirvana, and so on, as well as instructions on meditation and guidelines for ethical restraint. These were particularly popular among Taoist groups and for some time Buddhism and Taoism remained mixed together. With the introduction of the *Perfection of Wisdom* teachings, though, the Chinese were confronted with the Mahayana ("Greater Vehicle") tradition that claimed to offer a deeper and broader understanding of Buddhism than its predecessors, pejoratively labeled the Hinayana ("Lesser Vehicle"). Over the centuries that followed it was the Mahayana teachings that gained a wider acceptance among the Chinese. Schools were founded around famous Mahayana texts such as the *Mahaparinirvana Sutra,* the *Lotus Sutra,* the *Avatamsaka Sutra,* and the writings of the Madhyamika philosophers. Yet there was tremendous diversity in the ferment of Buddhist activity of these times. As late as the T'ang era (618–907) a Vinaya school was created emphasizing the monastic rule laid down by the early Indian traditions, as was a school based on the *Abhidharmakosha,* a Sarvastivadin work of Vasubandhu. A tantric school also flourished during the T'ang period but did not survive for long, although the Japanese Shingon sect still preserves some of its teachings today.

The Mahayana appealed to the Chinese because of its willingness to explore philosophical issues such as the nature of emptiness, an idea which strongly resonated with the Taoist notion of non-being; its offering of greater spiritual opportunities to the lay person, as exemplified by the bodhisattva Vimalakirti, an especially attractive figure for the Chinese literate gentry; its exotic symbolism and imagery, which provided more scope for the stimulation of the Chinese imagination; and its greater flexibility in adapting Buddhism to Chinese literary and other cultural forms. One should also remember that it had the advantages of freshness and novelty, for it arrived in China during the course of its development in India and was fervently espoused by missionaries in the full thrall of the creation of a new religious movement.

In the West we are receiving forms of both Theravada and Mahayana Buddhism that have changed little over the past few centuries. In many respects it has been the inspirational vitality of the individual proponents of these traditions rather than particular features of the traditions themselves that has been responsible for the flourishing of a certain order. One thinks of D.T. and Shunryu Suzuki in the case of Zen, and Chögyam Trungpa, Lama Yeshe and others in the case of Tibetan Buddhism. It is unclear whether native teachers of comparable stature have yet appeared. The little influence Buddhism has had in the cultural sphere has mainly stemmed from Mahayana sources: Zen in the visual arts and poetry, Madhyamika and Avatamsaka thought in philosophy and science. Again it must be emphasized that we are still at a very preliminary and preparatory stage in the introduction of Buddhism to the West. In all other instances in the past it has required centuries of domestication before the native genius was able to express itself in a mature Buddhist voice. In China the great figures of Chih I, Fa Tsang and Hui Neng only arose four or five hundred years after the introduction of the religion; likewise in Tibet, Milarepa, Sakya Pandita, Longchenpa and Tsongkhapa appeared after a similar period.

TRANSLATION

The effective communication of Buddhist ideas to an alien culture requires the process of translation, the skillful use of language being a vital key to unlock the prejudices of the mind against the threat of something new. Views about the way to translate Buddhist texts into Chinese evolved in a fashion that proves quite revealing in the light of current controversies about Buddhist translation in the West. Initially, the Buddhists adopted terms from indigenous Chinese thought in order to make their ideas comprehensible to the Chinese. The word *tao* was used to render at least three Sanskrit terms: *dharma, bodhi,* and *yoga. Chen-jen,* a Taoist term meaning "an immortal," was used to translate *arhat. Nirvana* was conveyed through another Taoist term, *wu-wei,* "non-activity." And *sila* was conveyed by the Confucian concept hsiao-hsün—"filial submission and obedience."[4] This approach was criticized by later translators because of the strong non-Buddhist associations brought to the Buddhist terms. Finally, it was felt preferable simply to transcribe the principal terms into Chinese. Thus *bodhi* became *bo-ri, arhat* became *a-lo-han, dhyana* became *ch'an, nirvana* became *nieh-pan,* and so on.[5] This may well prove to be the most effective way of rendering those key, multi-faceted

Buddhist concepts into English, about which translators seem incapable of agreeing upon a uniform rendition.

A further controversy arose between those translators, such as An Shih Kao and Chih Ch'an, who advocated a literal, word for word translation of the original, and others, such as Chih Ch'ien and Dharmaraksha, who preferred a fine, literary style at the expense of exact but often clumsy literalness.[6] The eminent fourth century Chinese monk Tao An argued at length on this conflict and concluded that although translation presented complex difficulties, it was necessary to keep as close as possible to the Sanskrit.[7] But, ironically, it was the person Tao An, encouraged to come to China as a translator, who finally decided the outcome of this controversy. This was the brilliant Kuchan translator Kumarajiva who arrived in Ch'ang-an at the turn of the fifth century. Kumarajiva disagreed with Tao An and emphasized that conveying the meaning of the original was more important than preserving its literal form. Style, he concluded, was important in communicating Buddhism to a literate Chinese audience, and where necessary, texts should be abbreviated and paraphrased.[8] Tao An and Kumarajiva did, however, agree that Taoist terminology had to be relinquished. For twelve years Kumarajiva and his team of Chinese collaborators systematically produced a wealth of remarkable translations of Mahayana writings, establishing the standard for the Chinese Buddhist canon as a whole.

We must recognize that it was not merely the method of translation but Kumarajiva's genius in applying it that resulted in these definitive Chinese versions of the Buddhist texts. To capture the spirit of Buddhism in words requires not only a knowledge of the languages involved, but a depth of understanding derived from a committed practice of the religion combined with a keen sensitivity to the cultural values of those one is addressing. Modern technology perhaps enables us to work more efficiently at the task of translation; the Chinese were hindered by the simple lack of communication between the different groups involved in the work. But no matter how literally exact a translation may be, if it fails to capture the imagination and quicken the spirit of the reader, it will serve as no more than a technical manual. For Buddhism to have a lasting impact on Western culture, it needs to create a "literature of spiritual conviction" (Yeats) that speaks in the terms of that culture.

Objections to Buddhism

By the eighth century, seven hundred years after its introduction, Buddhism reached the peak of its influence in China. In the words of Arthur F. Wright, "Buddhism was fully and triumphantly established throughout China. Its canons were revered, its spiritual truth unquestioned. It marked and influenced the lives of the humble and the great and affected every community, large and small, in the empire of T'ang."[9] But this glory was short-lived—in the ninth century the state began to turn against Buddhism and in 845 a decree was issued to suppress the religion. It never fully recovered from this persecution and its history from then until today has been one of decline. Although it continued to exert an influence in the arts and other areas of cultural life, with individual schools continuing to prosper, its authority in the minds of the Chinese was overshadowed by a revived form of Confucianism.

One of the main objections to Buddhism in China, which had been voiced in varying degrees ever since its introduction, was that it was a foreign religion alien to the spiritual life of China. Even in its most Chinese manifestations, it still bore the stigma of being founded by a non-Chinese, worshipping non-Chinese gods, and preaching a view of the world and society that went against many deeply-engrained Chinese values. When looking for a scapegoat at times of turmoil, it was always fairly easy to rally the emotions of the Chinese against the foreign religion of Buddhism.

Such arguments have also been put forward recently by eminent representatives of Western culture. Martin Heidegger maintained that a non-Western religion was incapable of resolving the crisis in Western culture—he believed that we had to find that resolution in a radical return to the origins of Western thought, in particular the pre-Socratic philosophers, a view similar in kind to that of the neo-Confucianists of ninth century China.[10] On psychological grounds, C.G. Jung has argued that it is actually dangerous for Westerners to attempt spiritual practices from the East, because they operate through symbols that are essentially foreign to our collective, cultural consciousness. Jung insisted that we had to rediscover our own symbols, unearth them from the obscure depths of our own unconscious. It is hard to judge to what extent such views are based upon irrational prejudice and to what extent they describe real difficulties in achieving genuine cross-cultural exchange. The Chinese experience with Buddhism would indicate that although a foreign religion can provide a valuable input of fresh ideas and symbols to help an established culture steer its way through a period of crisis, eventually those ideas and symbols will be appropriated by a renewed manifestation of the indigenous culture.

Another recurrent criticism of Buddhism in China was that it was an asocial religion concerned merely with the plight of the individual and indifferent to the state of society. The neo-Confucianists were highly critical of the Buddhist teachings on the empty, illusory, and transient nature of the world, arguing that they led to the weakening of political institutions, and offered no resistance to tyranny and corruption. A thousand years before Marx and Mao, the neo-Confucianist Ou Yang compared Buddhism to a drug which rendered the people insensible and enslaved.[11] To counteract the attraction of Buddhism, the neo-Confucianists evolved a view of life which both revived the traditional values of Confucius while introducing positive metaphysical and moral notions—such as that of *li*, the ultimate principle of reason that governs the life of the universe and man.[12] Although critical of Buddhism, the neo-Confucianists derived much of their inspiration from Buddhism itself. Their more sophisticated philosophical system, the broader sweep of their ethical concerns, and their use of meditation, all had their origins in the despised foreign religion.

Buddhism also attracts this kind of criticism in the West today. Its followers are accused of opting out of social and political responsibility, of succumbing to despair about the state of the world instead of rising to action, of tacitly supporting unjust government policies by refusing to speak out against them, of not translating their avowed ideals of love and compassion into deeds which will actually transform the world they live in. This has led to considerable soul-searching among certain Buddhists, some of whom have adopted a more outspoken stand on political and social issues. But I would guess that a significant number of modern Buddhists in the West do believe that a sane and just ordering of the world (*samsara*) is a hopeless endeavor, doomed from the outset, and that it is far more realistic to aim at a small degree of change within one's own consciousness and immediate social circle as the only genuine contribution to the betterment of life as a whole.

Arthur F. Wright speaks of four stages in the history of Buddhism in China: preparation, domestication, independent growth, and appropriation.[13] After its period of vigorous independent growth during the T'ang dynasty, Buddhism was appropriated as a part of Chinese culture, which, in a wave of resurgence, absorbed it into itself. Yet this resurgent Chinese culture was not a pristine Confucianist/Taoist phenomenon, standing proudly on its feet again to overthrow a now corrupt and discredited foreign religion. This Chinese culture was one renewed, expanded, and transformed by what Buddhism had injected into it. Hence much of what we perceive as Chinese today—the manner of the people, the art, the culture—reveals the legacy of Buddhist influence. A good example, again taken from Wright's book, is a statement by a leading Chinese Communist theorist describing the true party member as one who "grieves before all the rest of the

world grieves and is happy only after the rest of the world
is happy." This is simply a rephrasing of a neo-Confucianist
ideal appropriated from Mahayana Buddhism.[14]

A Second Renaissance?

I often wonder whether a similar process as occurred in
China will characterize the history of Buddhism in the
West. I remember being asked once whether I considered
myself to be a Westerner who had adopted Buddhism or
a Buddhist who happened to be reborn in the West. I am
still uncertain of the answer to this all important question,
but I have to admit that in many crucial respects I am first
and foremost a Westerner who has adopted Buddhism as a
means to come to terms with an existential crisis which, to
a large extent, is the outcome of a broader crisis within my
own culture. As a Buddhist, however, I feel uncomfortable
about this admission. There is clearly a conflict here which
must also have been experienced by the Chinese throughout
their involvement with Buddhism. This conflict, I believe,
lies at the root of all debates about the role of Buddhism in
the West and I am suspicious of anyone who claims to have
resolved it.

The idea that Buddhism may serve as a regenerative force
in Western culture has been expressed recently in the concept
of a second Renaissance: a Renaissance in which the spiritual
traditions of Asia are finally discovered and absorbed by the
West.[15] Such a process of discovery and regeneration would
be very similar to the "Renaissance" of the T'ang dynasty,
when Buddhism flourished in China much in the same way

as classical Greek culture flourished in medieval Europe. In this wider respect Buddhism would also act as a carrier of Asian cultures; indeed, one of its most valuable contributions to the West could be as the principal vehicle from the East capable of enriching our culture not merely with Buddhist values but also with traditional Indian, Chinese, Korean, Japanese, Vietnamese, Thai, Sri Lankan, and Tibetan traditional values. Although it is currently fashionable to imagine some kind of "essential Buddhism," stripped of all cultural packaging, as the only truly appropriate form of the religion for the West, I wonder whether such a culturally naked Buddhism is not an illusion—exactly the kind of illusion dispelled by the Madhyamika dialectic of Nagarjuna.

In the final analysis there is no entity called "Buddhism" which travels from one culture to another. The insights and values of Buddhism are transmitted solely through their being realized in and communicated through the lives of individual women and men.

And we can no more create a Western form of Buddhism than we can manufacture a fairy tale or a myth. For Buddhism achieves its cultural expressions in a mysterious and unpredictable way over many generations; in a way that no one of us can possibly foresee.

Afterword

I remained in Songgwang Sa until the first anniversary of Kusan Sŭnim's death, which took the form of a solemn ceremony in December 1984. By then Ilgak Sŭnim, a dharmabrother of Kusan whom none of the foreign monks or nuns knew, had been appointed Sŏn Master. Ilgak was a fine monk and competent teacher but he was not Kusan. I had the impression that he was appointed to the post because of his seniority in the Songgwang Sa monastic "family" rather than for any particular qualities as a man of the Way. The day after the ceremony, I left Korea for Hong Kong, returned my monastic vows and settled in a lay-Buddhist community in England. I would not set foot on the Korean peninsula again for another twenty-nine years.

The Korea to which I returned in October 2013 had changed almost beyond recognition. A third-world military dictatorship, still struggling to recover socially and economically from more than three decades of Japanese colonial occupation and the devastation of the Korean War, had been transformed into a first-world democracy and economic power-house with one of the highest standards of living on the planet. Some of this wealth had been used to improve

and expand the facilities of Buddhist monasteries. On reaching Songgwang Sa, I discovered that there was nothing left
of the physical meditation hall in which I had trained. It had
been demolished and entirely rebuilt on the same site. The
altar with the seated statue of Manjushri and the dusty cloth
bag was gone. The weathered painting of the Guardian
Kings, which hung outside above the wooden walkway, had
been taken to the new museum for safe-keeping. Instead of
the great stone tank fed by a single pipe of trickling water
from the mountain stood a gleaming modern bathhouse.

And there were no foreign monks or nuns undergoing
Sŏn training anymore. Since I left, the rules of admission
have changed. In order to enter the meditation hall today,
one has first to spend three years in a Sutra school studying
classical Buddhist discourses and Sŏn records. For a for-
eigner, this entails mastering spoken Korean and learning
enough classical Chinese to follow the teachings and write
the exam papers. Had such constraints been in place in 1981,
it is unlikely that I would have considered going to Korea at
all. For having spent eight years studying Buddhist theory
in Tibetan, my sole interest in coming to Songgwang Sa
at that time was to devote myself to long periods of silent
meditation.

Upon the death of Ilgak Sŭnim, the monk who succeeded
Kusan, Posŏng Sŭnim, who, in my day, was the Vinaya Master at the monastery, was appointed Sŏn Master. He is now
extremely old and frail. Although he seemed to recognize
me, I later learned that his attendant had to explain to him
in advance who I was. The other monks spoke in deferential
but urgent tones about the transition that will occur at his

passing and who is most likely to succeed him. There are a number of contending factions, each with its own candidate. Posŏng may be the last of Kusan's generation to hold this post. The next Sŏn master is likely to come from the generation of Kusan's disciples, i.e. monks of my own age whom I befriended when I lived in the monastery. Now in their sixties, they have earned the respect of their peers and are poised to assume a role that would mark the pinnacle of their monastic careers.

Most of Kusan Sŭnim's *sarira*—the mineral-like droplets we recovered from his cremation fire—are now enshrined in an elaborate granite memorial in a garden on the hillside next to Songgwang Sa. His passing is still mourned each December. The grandeur of the shrine stands in contrast to my memories of the simplicity of the man. He would have been embarrassed, I suspect, to be honored in death by a memorial more elegant and conspicuous than that of his own teacher Hyŏbong Sŭnim.

I became far more conscious during this return visit of the role that Kusan played in the restoration of the Sŏn monastic tradition in Korea after the end of the Japanese occupation in 1945. As part of their policy to incorporate Korean Buddhism into the Soto school of Zen, the colonial authorities had encouraged Korean monks to marry and have families as was the case in Japan. When Korea recovered its independence, the remaining celibate monks sought to remove all married priests from the monasteries and restore the Vinaya-based tradition. I knew that Kusan had played a role in this movement, but had not been aware that he had penned a declaration of resolve in his own blood, which was displayed as a banner in public demonstrations to demand the return of the monasteries.

Kusan's uncompromising fierceness as a Sŏn master was thus mirrored in his political activism in the 1950's. I realize now that he was honored with such a grand memorial not only because of his spiritual achievements but for the crucial part he played in the post-colonial struggle with the married clergy.

As for myself, on leaving Songgwang Sa after four years of Sŏn training, I subsequently married Songil (Martine Fages), a former nun and disciple of Kusan to whom this book is dedicated. Kusan would have deplored this had he still been alive—though in my mind I can hear him chuckle at the irony of it as well. After all he had been through, he was no stranger to the quirks and passions of humankind. He tended to spare his ferocity for his Korean disciples, and was remarkably tolerant and forgiving towards us foreigners.

On settling in Europe, my interests turned more towards the early teachings of the Buddha as recorded in the Pali canon. I did not reject the teachings of Sŏn, but sought to integrate them in a broader synthesis of Buddhism as a way of life adapted to the demands of secular modernity. Since we left the monastery, Martine and I have faithfully conducted one week-long Sŏn retreat a year, based on the same format and schedule as the training we received at Songgwang Sa. We may not start each day at 3 AM nor sit for as long as we did in Korea, but the practice of "What is this?" remains at the core of what we teach. We likewise incorporate the exercise of this radical questioning into all the other retreats that we lead every year in different parts of the world.

In the light of my departure from Sŏn Buddhist ortho-
doxy, not to mention my marriage to a former nun, I was
greatly moved by the generosity and kindness of the monks
I met on my return to Korea after such a long absence. Once
one has been accepted into the "family" of a Korean monastery, one always remains part of that family, irrespective of
anything else one may have done.

I was also struck by how many Korean monastics today are
exploring other schools and teachings of Buddhism. South
Korea's new-found prosperity has enabled some monks and
nuns to practice in Theravāda monasteries in Burma and
Tibetan centres in India, or pursue university degrees in the
West in order to deepen their understanding of the Dharma.
It would be premature to speculate about how this expo-
sure to the wider Buddhist tradition might affect the future
development of Korean Sŏn, but it suggests a healthy openness to difference and a willingness to embrace the kinds of
change that appear inevitable as Buddhism engages with the
challenges of the contemporary world.

2014

Notes

Chapter One—Question and Response

1. Such exhortations are not merely symbolic. Zen students may actually be encouraged to place their questioning in the belly. This passage comes from Wu Men's commentary to the first case in the *Gateless Gate (Wumenkuan)*, Chao Chou's "No!" ("Wu"). Quoted in Roshi Philip Kapleau. *The Three Pillars of Zen*, p. 76.
2. This is the forty-second case of the *Blue Cliff Record*. From Thomas and J.C. Cleary. *The Blue Cliff Record*, p. 301.
3. Chandrakirti. *A Guide to the Middle Way (Madhyamakavatara)*: I: 18.
4. Shantideva. *A Guide to the Bodhisattva's Way of Life (Bodhicaryavatara)*: VIII: 116.
5. T.S. Eliot. *East Coker*, line 189. From *Four Quartets*, p. 31.

Chapter Two—The Faith to Doubt

1. Walpola Rahula. *What the Buddha Taught*, p. 109.
2. *Ibid.*, pp. 2-3.
3. Martin Buber. *I and Thou*, pp. 83-4.
4. Keiji Nishitani. *Religion and Nothingness*, p. 20.
5. *Ibid.*, p. 16.

Chapter Three—What Is It?

1. John R. McRae. *The Northern School and the Formation of Early Ch'an Buddhism*, p. 92. I have taken a liberty with chronology here.

McRae's excellent book was not published until after my return from Korea to England.

2. *Ibid.*, P. 92.

3. *Ibid.*, p. 92.

4. Cf. Lu K'uan Yü. *The Transmission of the Mind outside the Teaching*, p. 33; Fung and Fung. *The Sutra of the Sixth Patriarch on the Pristine Orthodox Dharma*, pp. 102-3; and Robert Buswell. *The Korean Approach to Zen: The Collected Works of Chinul*, p. 335. The encounter between Huai Jang and Hui Neng only appears in the later editions of the *Platform Sutra*. This episode as well as any mention of Huai Jang is absent from the earliest known edition of the text found among the Tun Huang manuscripts. See Philip Yampolsky. *The Platform Sutra of the Sixth Patriarch*, p. 53.

5. Cf. Lu K'uan Yü. *Ibid.*, p. 37.

6. Chang Chung-yülan. *Original Teachings of Ch'an Buddhism*, p. 149.

7. *Ibid.*, p. 150. Also cf. Lu K'uan Yü. *Op. cit.*, p. 44.

8. *Ibid.*, pp. 153-4.

9. Thomas Cleary. *The Sayings and Doings of Pai Chang*, p. 27. *Also cf.* Lu K'uan Yü. *Op. cit.*, p. 50.

10. Cf. Thomas Cleary. *Op. cit.*, p. 17 and p. 27, and Thomas and J.C. Cleary. *Op. cit.*, p. 357.

11. Thomas Cleary. *Op. cit.*, p. 21. *Also cf.* Lu K'uan Yü. *Op. cit.*, p. 57.

12. John Blofeld. *The Zen Teaching of Huang Po*, pp. 37-8.

13. *Ibid.*, p. 35.

14. *Ibid.*, p. 93.

15. Cf. Ruth F. Sasaki. *The Record of Lin Chi*, p. 3; T.P. Kasulis. *Zen Action, Zen Person*, p. 51; Irmgard Schloegl. *The Zen Teaching of Rinzai*, p. 15; and Lu K'uan Yü. *Ch'an and Zen Teachings: Second Series*, p. 110.

16. Cf. Chang Chung-yülan. *Op. cit.*, pp. 111-2.

17. Cf. Thomas and J.C. Cleary. *Op. cit.*, pp. 37-8, and Lu K'uan Yü. *Ch'an and Zen Teachings: Second Series*, pp. 181-2. In the text Yun Men replies to Mu Chou's question "Who's there?" with his personal name "Wen Yen." For the sake of clarity I have substituted "Yun Men," even though he would not have used this name of himself.

18. Thomas and J.C. Cleary. *Op. cit.*, pp. 146-7.

19. Cf. *Ibid.*, p. 345 and 347.
20. *Ibid.*, p. 243. The disciple's name was Hui Leng (846-932).
21. *Ibid.*, p. 243.
22. *Ibid.*, p. 38.
23. *Ibid.*, p. 289.
24. *Ibid.*, p. 111.
25. Christopher Cleary. *Swampland Flowers: The Letters and Lectures of Zen Master Ta Hui*, p. 75.

CHAPTER FOUR—QUESTIONING

1. Martin Heidegger. *Discourse on Thinking: A Translation of Gelassenheit.* p. 46. Calculative thinking *(rechnendes Denken)* and meditative thinking *(besinnliches Denken)* are the two principal themes running through the first part of this short book, the *Memorial Address.* Meditative thinking "demands of us not to cling one-sidedly to a single idea, nor to run down a one-track course of ideas. Meditative thinking demands of us that we engage ourselves with what at first sight does not go together at all." (p. 53) Heidegger regards calculative thinking as dangerous insofar that it "may someday come to be accepted and practiced as the only way of thinking." (p. 56) If this were to happen "then man would have denied and thrown away his own special nature—that he is a meditative being. Therefore, the issue is the saving of man's essential nature. Therefore, the issue is keeping meditative thinking alive." (p. 56)
2. The distinction between problem and mystery follows Gabriel Marcel's *Being and Having: An Existentialist Diary.* The notion of mystery is also influenced by Heidegger's treatment of the subject in his *Discourse on Thinking.* In Marcel's thought, problem and mystery are correlated to the categories of having and being, objectification and participation, abstraction and concrete thinking, respectively. (See Sam Keen. *Gabriel Marcel*, p. 14.) Here I have also correlated the Heideggerian polarities of calculative and meditative thinking with Marcel's notion of problem and mystery. A consideration of the problem-oriented, calculating, abstract, possessive, and objectifying attitude led both of these thinkers to further analyze the meaning and role of technology. See Heidegger's *The Question of*

Technology (Basic Writings, pp. 283-317) and Marcel's *Man Against Mass Society*.

3. *Cf.* Heidegger. *The Discourse on Thinking, p. 45.*

4. *Ibid.,* p. 55.

5. Hsü Yün (1840-1959) is regarded as the greatest Chinese Ch'an (Zen) master of recent times. For an account of his life see *Empty Cloud: The Autobiography of the Chinese Zen Master Xu Yun.* An extensive selection of his teachings is presented in Lu K'uan Yü. *Ch'an and Zen Teaching: First Series*, pp. 16-117.

6. Arthur Waley. *The Way and Its Power: A Study of the Tao Te Ching and Its Place in Chinese Thought*, p. 197. (*Tao Te Ching*: 43)

7. *Ibid.,* p. 151 (*Tao Te Ching*: 8).

8. Gabriel Marcel. *Being and Having: An Existentialist Diary*, p. 117.

9. Concerning "Great Doubt," Keiji Nishitani explains: "Its characterization as 'Great' seems to hinge, for one thing, on the content of the doubt itself. The very condition of basic uncertainty regarding human existence in the world and the existence of self and others, as well as the suffering that this gives rise to, are surely matters of the utmost, elemental concern. As the Chinese adage has it, 'Birth and death—the great matter.' The word 'Great,' then, may also be said to refer to the consciousness of our mode of being and way of existing in response to this 'great matter'." (*Religion and Nothingness,* p. 16)

10. Philip Yampolsky. *The Platform Sutra of the Sixth Patriarch*, p. 138.

11. Cited in T.P. Kasulis. *Zen Action, Zen Person*, p. 44.

12. Philip Yampolsky. *Op. cit.,* p. 138.

13. Christopher Cleary. *Op. cit.*, p. 48.

14. Cf. Martin Heidegger. *Discourse on Thinking: A Translation of Gelassenheit,* p. 68: "*Teacher:* Waiting, all right, but never expecting, for expecting already links itself with representing and what is represented." To preserve the literal proximity between the German *Warten* (waiting) and *Erwarten* (expecting), the translators of *Gelassenheit* used "waiting" and "awaiting" respectively. I have changed the latter term to "expecting" since "awaiting" fails to convey what is entailed in expectation.

15. This is admittedly a general distinction based only on the habitual manner of looking and listening. Through training, looking too can be made to perceive in a more meditative fashion.

16. Diane Wolkstein and Samuel Noah Kramer. *Innana: Queen of Heaven and Earth*, p. xvii. This reference was given to me by Mr. Richard Gassner.

17. Lu K'uan Yü. *The Surangama Sutra*, p. 142.

18. *Ibid.*, p. 147. Hsü Yün explains this further in Lu K'uan Yü. *Ch'an and Zen Teaching: First Series*, pp. 89-93.

19. Marie-Louise von Franz. *Puer Aeternus*, p. 94.

20. See above (*The Faith to Doubt*). p. 27.

21. Thomas and J.C. Cleary. *Op. cit.*, p. 235.

22. Cf. the discussion of the koan by Chung Feng Ming Pen (1263-1323) as translated by Isshu Miura and Ruth Fuller Sasaki in *The Zen Koan: Its History and Use in Rinzai Zen*, pp. 4-7.

23. Cf. Kusan Sunim. *The Way of Korean Zen*, p. 61.

24. Cited in Masao Abe. *Zen and Western Thought*, p. 37.

25. *Ibid.*, p. 37.

26. Of the hundred cases in the *Blue Cliff Record* five are drawn from the Indian sutras. Two of these cases (nos. 78 and 94) refer to incidents in the *Shurangama Sutra;* one (no. 84) to an episode in the *Vimalakirti Sutra;* and one (no. 97) to a statement from the *Diamond Sutra*. The ninety-second case does not clearly belong to any sutra. It simply says: "One day the World Honored One ascended his seat. Manjushri struck the gavel and said, 'Clearly behold the Dharma of the King of Dharma; the Dharma of the King of Dharma is thus.' The World Honored One then got down off his seat." (Thomas and J.C. Cleary. *Op. cit.*, p. 588.)

27. There are numerous translations of this sutra. Here I follow the version in Geshé Rabten. *Echoes of Voidness*, pp. 18-9.

28. It could be argued that forsaking the genre in which the *Heart Sutra* has been traditionally presented necessarily compromises the meaning of the text as a whole. It is open to question whether the full meaning of a classical discourse such as this is "paraphrasable in a series of propositions that claim to say the same thing." (David Tracy. *The Analogical Imagination*, p. 127.)

29. Cf. Thomas Merton. *Contemplative Prayer*, p. 32: "In proportion as meditation takes on a more contemplative character, we see that it is not only a means to an end, but also has something of the nature of an end." Elsewhere in this book Merton goes on to say: "In meditation we should not look for a 'method' or 'system,' but cultivate an

'attitude,' an 'outlook': faith, reverence, expectation, supplication, trust, joy. All these finally permeate our being with love insofar as our living faith tells us . . . that in the Spirit of God we 'see' God our Father without 'seeing.' We know him in 'unknowing.'" (p. 39) Although Merton speaks of a meditative attitude as characterized by not-seeing and unknowing, he nonetheless considers expectation to be one of its qualities.

CHAPTER SIX—UNPREDICTABLE MOMENTS

1. Lao Tzu. *Tao Te Ching*: 29. From Arthur Waley. *Op. cit.*, p. 179.
2. Gabriel Marcel. *Man Against Mass Society*, p. 99. "A world where techniques . . . to serve some desire or fear" is from *Being and Having: An Existentialist Diary*, p. 76.
3. Martin Buber. *I and Thou*, p. 82.
4. Ta Hui. Quoted in Chinul's *Excerpts from the Dharma Collection*. From Robert Buswell. *The Korean Approach to Zen: The Collected Works of Chinul*, pp. 337-8.
5. Hui Neng. *The Platform Sutra*. From Philip Yampolsky. *The Platform Sutra of the Sixth Patriarch*, pp. 151 and 179.
6. Ta Hui. From Christopher Cleary. *Op. cit.*, p. 13.
7. *Ibid.*, p. 71.
8. Hui Neng. Quoted in Chinul's *Excerpts from the Dharma Collection*. From Buswell. *Op. cit.*, pp. 334-5. In Chinul's text this dialogue between Hui Neng and Shen Hui and the exchange with Huai Jang are cited together to illustrate the same point. As with the Huai Jang episode, this dialogue is not included in the earlier Tun Huang text of the *Platform Sutra*.
9. Martin Buber. *Op. cit.*, pp. 83-4.
10. Li T'ung Hsüan. *Exposition of the Avatamsaka Sutra*. Quoted in Chinul's *Complete and Sudden Attainment of Buddhahood*. From Buswell. *Op. cit.*, p. 223. Li T'ung Hsüan (635-730) was a Chinese commentator on Hua Yen philosophy. Although his work had little influence in China during his lifetime, it played a significant role in the development of Buddhist thought in Korea and Japan.
11. T. S. Eliot. *East Coker,* lines 123-8. *Four Quartets*, p. 28.
12. Li T'ung Hsüan. *Exposition of the Avatamsaka Sutra*. Quoted in

Chinul's *Complete and Sudden Attainment of Buddhahood*. From Buswell. *Op. cit.*, p. 204.

13. Takasui. Quoted in Keiji Nishitani. *Religion and Nothingness*, p. 20.

14. Meister Eckhart. From Reiner Schürmann. *Meister Eckhart: Mystic and Philosopher*, p. 7.

15. Gabriel Marcel. *Man Against Mass Society*, pp. 189-90.

16. Yung Ming Yen Shou. *The Mirror of the Source Record*. Quoted in Chinul's *Excerpts from the Dharma Collection*. From Buswell. *Op. cit.*, p. 325. Yung Ming Yen Shou (904-975) was a Chinese Zen monk who advocated a rapprochement between the contemplative and scholastic traditions of Buddhism.

17. Gabriel Marcel. *Being and Having: An Existentialist Diary*, p. 48. Marcel concludes this passage on a rather dour note: "I must accept this fact with shame and sorrow."

18. Chuang Tzu. From Burton Watson. *Chuang Tzu: Basic Writings*, p. 54.

19. Ch'eng Kuan. *Essentials of the Hua Yen Teaching*. Quoted in Chinul's *Excerpts from the Dharma Collection*. From Buswell. *Op. cit.*, p. 328. Ch'eng Kuan (738-840) was the fourth patriarch of the Chinese Hua Yen school of Buddhism.

20. Uisang. *Chart of the Avatamsaka's One Vehicle Dharmadhatu*. Quoted in Chinul's *Excerpts from the Dharma Collection*. From Buswell. *Op. cit.*, p. 326. Uisang (625-702) was the founder of the Korean Hwaom (Hua Yen) school of Buddhism.

Appendix—The Chinese Lesson

1. Kenneth Ch'en. *Buddhism in China: A Historical Survey*, pp. 114-5, 128-9.

2. Arthur F. Wright. *Buddhism in Chinese History*, p. 41.

3. *Ibid.*, p. 57.

4. *Ibid.*, p. 36.

5. Ch'en. *Op. cit.*, p. 372 n.

6. *Ibid.*, p. 369.

7. *Ibid.*, pp. 370-1.

8. *Ibid.*, pp. 371-2.

9. Wright. *Op. cit.*, pp. 82-3.

10. See *Nur ein Gott Kann Uns Retten*, an interview printed in the year of Heidegger's death in the magazine *Der Spiegel*, XXIII (1976).

11. Wright. *Op. cit.*, p. 88.

12. Ch'en. *Op. cit.*, pp. 396-7.

13. Wright. *Op. cit.*, passim.

14. *Ibid.*, pp. 122-3.

15. See Robert A.F. Thurman. *Tsong Khapa's Speech of Gold in the Essence of True Eloquence*, p.111; Sangharakshita. *The Glory of the Literary World*, pp. 1-2; and Maurice Ash. *New Renaissance*, pp. 7-10.

Bibliography

Abe, Masao. Ed. William R. Lafleur. *Zen and Western Thought.* Honolulu: University of Hawaii Press, 1985.

Ash, Maurice. *New Renaissance.* Hartland, U.K.: Green Books, 1987.

Barrett, William. *The Illusion of Technique: A Search for the Meaning of Life in a Technological Age.* New York: Doubleday, 1979.

Batchelor, Stephen. *Alone With Others: An Existential Approach to Buddhism.* New York: Grove Press, 1983.

Blofeld, John. *The Zen Teaching of Huang Po.* New York: Grove Press, 1958.

Buber, Martin. Tr. Walter Kaufmann. *I and Thou.* New York: Charles Scribner's, 1970.

Buswell, Robert. *The Korean Approach to Zen: The Collected Works of Chinul.* Honolulu: University of Hawaii Press, 1983.

Chandrakirti. *A Guide to the Middle Way (Madhyamakavatara).* No. 5262, Vol. 98 of the Peking Edition of the Tibetan Tripitaka. Tokyo/ Kyoto: The Suzuki Research Foundation, 1956. Translated in part in Geshé Rabten. *Echoes of Voidness.* (See below.)

Chang Chung-Yuan. *Original Teachings of Ch'an Buddhism.* New York: Grove Press, 1982.

Ch'en, Kenneth. *Buddhism in China: A Historical Survey.* Princeton: Princeton University Press, 1964.

Cleary, Christopher. *Swampland Flowers: The Letters and Lectures of Zen Master Ta Hui.* New York: Grove Press, 1977.

Cleary, Thomas. *Sayings and Doings of Pai Chang.* Los Angeles: Center Publications, 1978.

Cleary, Thomas and Cleary, J.C. *The Blue Cliff Record* (3 Vols.) Boulder: Shambhala, 1977.

Eliot, T. S. *Four Quartets.* Orlando: Harcourt, Brace, Jovanovich, 1988.

Fung and Fung. *The Sutra of the Sixth Patriarch on the Pristine Orthodox Dharma.* San Francisco: Buddha's Universal Church, 1964.

Heidegger, Martin. Ed. David Farrell Krell. *Basic Writings.* New York: Harper & Row, 1977.

————. Tr. John M. Anderson and E. Hans Freund. *Discourse on Thinking: A Translation of Gelassenheit.* New York: Harper & Row, 1966.

Kapleau, Roshi Philip. *The Three Pillars of Zen.* New York: Doubleday, 1965.

Kasulis, T.P. *Zen Action, Zen Person.* Honolulu: University of Hawaii Press, 1981.

Keen, Sam. *Gabriel Marcel.* Richmond: John Knox Press, 1967.

Kusan Sunim. Tr. Martine Fages. Ed. Stephen Batchelor. *The Way of Korean Zen.* Tokyo/New York: Weatherhill, 1985.

————. Tr. Hae Myong Sunim (Robert Buswell) and Hae Haeng Sunim (Renaud Neubauer). *Nine Mountains.* Korea: Songgwang Sa Monastery, 1976.

Lu K'uan Yü (Charles Luk). *Ch'an and Zen Teaching: First Series.* London: Rider, 1960.

————. *Ch'an and Zen Teaching: Second Series.* London: Rider, 1961.

————. *Ch'an and Zen Teaching: Third Series.* London: Rider, 1962.

————. *The Transmission of the Mind Outside the Teaching.* London: Rider, 1974.

————. *The Surangama Sutra.* London: Rider, 1966.

Marcel, Gabriel. *Being and Having: An Existentialist Diary.* Gloucester, Mass.: Peter Smith, 1976.

————. *Man Against Mass Society.* South Bend: Gateway Editions, n.d.

McRae, John R. *The Northern School and the Formation of Early Ch'an Buddhism.* Honolulu: University of Hawaii Press, 1986.

Merton, Thomas. *Contemplative Prayer.* New York: Doubleday, 1971.

Miura, Isshu, and Sasaki, Ruth Fuller. *The Zen Koan: Its History and Use in Rinzai Zen.* New York: Harcourt, Brace and World, 1965.

Mu Soeng. *Thousand Peaks: Korean Zen—Tradition and Teachers.* Berkeley: Parallax Press, 1987.

Nishitani, Keiji. *Religion and Nothingness.* Berkeley: University of California Press, 1982.

Rabten, Geshé. Tr. Stephen Batchelor. *Echoes of Voidness.* Boston: Wisdom, 1983.

Rahula, Walpola. *What the Buddha Taught.* New York: Grove Press, 1974.

Sangharakshita. *The Glory of the Literary World.* Glasgow. Windhorse, 1985.

Sasaki, Ruth F. *The Record of Lin-Chi.* Kyoto: Institute for Zen Studies, 1975.

Schloegl, Irmgard. *The Zen Teaching of Rinzai.* Berkeley: Shambhala, 1975.

Schürmann, Reiner. *Meister Eckhart: Mystic and Philosopher.* Bloomington: Indiana University Press, 1978.

Shantideva. Tr. Stephen Batchelor. *A Guide to the Bodhisattva's Way of Life (Bodhicaryavatara).* Dharamsala: The Library of Tibetan Works and Archives, 1979.

Thurman, Robert A.F. *Tsong Khapa's Speech of Gold in the Essence of True Eloquence.* Princeton: Princeton University Press, 1984.

Tracy, David. *The Analogical Imagination.* New York: Crossroad, 1981.

Von Franz, Marie-Louise. *Puer Aeternus.* Santa Monica: Sigo Press, 1981.

Waley, Arthur. *The Way and Its Power: A Study of the Tao Te Ching and Its Place in Chinese Thought.* New York: Grove Press, 1958.

Watson, Burton. *Chuang Tzu: Basic Writings.* New York: Columbia University Press, 1964.

Wolkstein, Diane, and Kramer, Samuel Noah. *Innana: Queen of Heaven and Earth.* New York: Harper & Row, 1983.

Wright, Arthur F. *Buddhism in Chinese History.* Stanford: Stanford University Press, 1959.

Xu Yun. Tr. Charles Luk. Ed. Richard Hunn. *Empty Cloud: The Autobiography of the Chinese Zen Master Xu Yun.* Shaftesbury, U.K.: Element, 1988.

Yampolsky, Philip B. *The Platform Sutra of the Sixth Patriarch.* New York: Columbia University Press, 1967.